SCHOOL LEADERSHIP
From A to Z

For Joyce, Jeff, Kim, Nathan, Dan, Adam, Maddie and Jo.

ROBERT D. RAMSEY

SCHOOL LEADERSHIP
From A to Z

Practical Lessons from Successful
Schools and Businesses

CORWIN PRESS, INC.
A Sage Publications Company
Thousand Oaks, California

For information:

Corwin Press, Inc.
A Sage Publications Company
2455 Teller Road
Thousand Oaks, California 91320
www.corwinpress.com

Sage Publications Ltd.
6 Bonhill Street
London EC2A 4PU
United Kingdom

Sage Publications India Pvt. Ltd.
B-42, Panchsheel Enclave
Post Box 4109
New Delhi 110 017 India

Printed in the United States of America

Library of Congress Cataloging-in-Publication Data

Ramsey, Robert D.
School leadership from A to Z: Practical lessons from successful schools and businesses / Robert D. Ramsey.
    p. cm.
Includes bibliographical references.
ISBN 0–7619–3832-X (Cloth)—ISBN 0–7619–3833–8 (Paper)
  1. Educational leadership—United States-Handbooks, manuals, etc. 2. School administrators—United States—Handbooks, manuals, etc. 3. School management and organization—United States—Handbooks, manuals, etc. I. Title.
LB2831.82.R37 2003
371.2—dc21

                                2003001193

03   04   05   06   10 9 8 7 6 5 4 3 2 1

Acquisitions Editor:	Robert D. Clouse
Associate Editor:	Kristen L. Gibson
Editorial Assistant:	Jingle Vea
Production Editor:	Melanie Birdsall
Typesetter:	C&M Digitals (P) Ltd.
Proofreader:	Ruth Saavedra
Cover Designer:	Tracy E. Miller
Production Artist:	Lisa Miller

Contents

Acknowledgments

Every worthwhile production has a talented supporting cast. Mine included a supporting and collaborative wife; a generous son and a confidant willing to share his personal library on leadership; an insightful and affirming editor (Robb Clouse); a host of effective educational leaders who have mentored and inspired me over the years (you know who you are); and countless business experts and writers who have helped me understand what it takes to lead today.

Without this cast, this production would never have come to fruition. There is no way to express adequate appreciation to all the supporting players. There is only "Thank you." So I'll simply say it. Thank you!—and I mean it.

Corwin Press would like to acknowledge the contributions of the following individuals:

Paul G. Young
President, NAESP Board of Directors
Principal
West Elementary School
Lancaster, OH

Bob Tift
President
Benilde-St. Margaret's School
St. Louis Park, MN

Patricia Kinney
MetLife/NASSP 2003 National Middle Level Principal of the Year
Principal
Talent Middle School
Talent, OR

Roger Hill
NAESP 2002 National Distinguished Principal
Principal
Birch Kirksey Middle School
Rogers, AR

Denny R. Vincent
President, NASSP Board of Directors
Principal
Muhlenberg North High School
Greenville, KY

Belinda S. Akin
NAESP 2002 National Distinguished Principal
Principal
Monticello Intermediate School
Monticello, AR

Donald Draayer
AASA 1990 Superintendent of the Year
Minnetonka, MN

About the Author

 **Robert D. Ramsey** is a lifelong educator who has served as a "leader of leaders" in three award-winning school districts in two states. His front-line experience includes positions as teacher, counselor, supervisor, assistant principal, curriculum coordinator, personnel director, associate superintendent, acting superintendent, and adjunct professor.

Ramsey now works full-time as a freelance writer in Minneapolis where he lives with his wife and is close to his children and grandchildren. He is the author of several successful books for educators and parents and is a frequent contributor to numerous popular journals and newspapers.

Throughout his distinguished career, Ramsey's writings have helped and inspired countless teachers and administrators to achieve greater success. His best-selling *Lead, Follow or Get Out of the Way* has been widely heralded as "must reading" for principals and superintendents.

In his latest work, *School Leadership From A to Z*, Ramsey again provides insights and inspiration that can help busy administrators translate the theories of leadership into here-and-now reality.

OTHER BOOKS BY ROBERT D. RAMSEY

The Principals' Book of Lists (Prentice-Hall)

Lead, Follow or Get Out of the Way (Corwin)

Fiscal Fitness for School Administrators (Corwin)

Well Said, Well Spoken: 736 Quotable Quotes for Educators (Corwin)

How to Say the Right Thing Every Time (Corwin)

501 Tips for Teachers (Contemporary Books)

Introduction

When you enter the workplace, you never leave it at zero. You either make it a little better or a little worse.

—Buckingham and Coffman
First, Break All the Rules

School leadership just isn't what it used to be. When French companies start offering back-to-school "bully insurance" to reimburse parents and pupils for property that is damaged or stolen by other kids and when the National Education Association (NEA) starts selling "homicide insurance," providing benefits to the families of teachers killed on the job, you know something is different.

Times change. Families change. Kids change. And schools change. Our world won't tolerate stationary entities. So school leaders have to change, too.

To survive and thrive as a principal or superintendent anymore, administrators have to learn new skills, invent new techniques, dust off some forgotten strategies and retrofit some others. That's where the little book you're holding comes in.

School Leadership From A to Z is a hard-hitting, hands-on guide for school officials offering a different look at what it takes to be an effective leader in today's schools. It covers every aspect of school leadership from A (Attitude and Ambiguity Tolerance) to Z (Zen for School Leaders) and everything in between.

And it does all this by combining the best thinking from today's best schools with proven ideas (which many educators don't know about or don't realize will work in schools) taken directly from successful businesses and other public and private organizations.

This is the first-ever handbook for educational leaders to draw heavily on tough lessons from business and life, as well as from successful school experiences.

As educators, we sometimes look down on and distance ourselves from the "crass" business community as if the business mentality is somehow inferior or beneath us. Likewise, we tend to think that what works for effective business leaders won't work with school personnel. Wrong on both counts!

These are self-defeating attitudes, which often rob educators of a rich resource for bettering our schools and becoming more effective school leaders. After all, if Bill Gates can't teach us something about how to get results, who can?

As it turns out, much of what makes a great business organization tick can help make an effective school click as well. Schools, businesses, and other organizations are more alike than we realize. ("The most important difference between business and academia is this: In business everything is dog eat dog. In academia it's just the opposite." —E. John Rosenwald Jr.) Schools can learn a lot from business. After all, your school is a business—and much more.

That's why this how-to guide blends proven traditional success secrets for school leaders with newfound strategies and fresh approaches taken directly from the nation's business and other public and private organizations outside the education community. Each section is packed with real-world tips and insights that can work in any school.

The following sections are full of trade secrets for modern-day principals and superintendents. From cover to cover, the text pinpoints the specific attitudes, attributes, roles, rules, and practices that boost the best administrators toward lasting success. It's not theory. It's just what works.

This fresh approach carries over into four resource sections: *A New Vocabulary for School Leaders; What Business Leaders Say About Leadership That School Leaders Need to Hear; Business Books You Might Want to Read to Become a Better School Leader;* and *Borrowing From Business—Bright Ideas You Can Use in Your School Starting Tomorrow Morning.* This extra material alone makes the book worthwhile reading for success-minded school leaders.

To facilitate quick reading and easy use, the guide is organized into 26 compact sections (one for each letter of the alphabet). Each section stands alone, offering provocative, insider insight into critical elements of school leadership. Together they cover everything it takes to run a school today. It's a different format that favors busy professionals. It's easy to read. And hard to forget.

Being a principal or superintendent is more difficult than it ever has been—and more important. That's why all school leaders need help, support, and backup today.

Sometimes the cavalry comes in the form of a small book with big ideas. Reading the following pages won't make your job as easy as A, B, C, but it will make it more manageable and more fun.

Of course, just mastering the letters of the alphabet won't guarantee that students will become great readers or writers, but it does give them a leg up. Likewise, mastering the tools and techniques in the succeeding sections won't ensure your success as a school administrator. But it will increase the odds in your favor and give you a real shot at lifting your school beyond the ordinary.

No real leader would ask for more.

A Attitude and Ambiguity Tolerance

You don't need experience if you've got attitude.

—Scott Adams, creator
Dilbert comic strip

It takes many different qualities, competencies, habits, and skills to be an effective leader in today's schools. This book is full of them. But it all starts with an attitude:

• Mike Hickey had it when he announced his retirement as superintendent of the Howard County (Maryland) Schools a full year in advance. When skeptics asked if he was worried about being a lame duck, Hickey replied, "No, because I'll be a lame duck with an attitude!" (You're a lame duck only if you allow yourself to limp along.)

• Carol Johnson, superintendent in Minneapolis, had an attitude when she turned down a hefty salary increase, insisting that the money go instead for underfinanced school programs.

• Owen Henson, principal in Topeka (Kansas), had an attitude when he waived traditional requirements so that a minority student could be the first member of his family to graduate from high school.

• Marvin Maire, superintendent in St. Louis Park (Minnesota), had an attitude when he was being hounded by a prominent citizen who demanded an inordinate amount of time, insisting, "I'm a taxpayer. You have to listen to me. I pay your salary." Finally, Maire handed the pest a dollar bill and said, "There's your share of my salary. We're even. Don't bother me any more!"

- We've all heard of principals who showed an attitude when they allowed their students to shave their heads or drench them in a dunk tank after their school reached ambitious reading goals.

It's true everywhere you look. The best school leaders have a little different attitude than most other people. But it's not the attitude you may expect.

If you assume that great leaders have a larger-than-life ego, a bombastic demeanor, and a charismatic, cocky attitude, you're way off the mark. As it turns out, lasting leaders have a lot less flamboyant attitude than some people think. There is a difference between a guiding light and a flash in the pan.

Think about the rise and fall of school leaders you have known. How many shooting stars have you watched burn out, never to be heard of again? How many gargantuan egos can you count that eventually became irrelevant as others grew weary of their overbearing attitude?

Great leaders—in schools, in businesses, anywhere—are sure of themselves without being full of themselves. They are self-confident without being self-centered. It's the difference between a confident stride and a swagger. And it's all a matter of attitude.

If you need convincing, check out the groundbreaking research of Jim Collins and his team of investigators who identified the distinguishing attitudes that set apart those business leaders whose companies achieve greatness (*From Good to Great: Why Some Companies Make the Leap and Others Don't*; see Resource 3).

Based on their findings, the leaders who build great organizations are more like "plow horses" than "show horses." In the long run, a charismatic attitude is just about style. True leadership is all about substance.

According to Collins, outstanding business leaders (he calls them "Level 5" leaders) demonstrate an attitude of genuine personal humility, coupled with a strong professional will to get things done no matter what it takes. They may be modest about their own accomplishments, but they have an outspoken, absolute faith in the organization's ability to prevail and an unswerving resolve to go to any limit to help their company get to the top and stay there.

Take another look around at your peers. Aren't these the same attitudes found in the best administrators you know? Why should we be surprised that what works in business works in schools as well?

Level 5 leaders give others credit while channeling their personal ambition into achieving collective success. They are doggedly determined, realistic (willing to face hard facts), and terminally optimistic about the certainty of ultimate triumph.

As educators, we don't run a business, but I'm pretty sure we all want this same kind of leader for our schools. Because they get results. Because they don't just settle for good (average is overrated) when greatness is a possibility. And because they have the "right attitude."

Some of your colleagues may think that attitude isn't such a big deal. Just as some people still think the earth is flat. It doesn't matter. You know better.

The truth is that the kind of school leader you are or will ever become begins and ends with your attitude. The leader you want to be

- *Has a "can-do" attitude.* Confidence gives you courage and extends your reach. It allows you to take reasonable risks and do more than you thought possible.

- *Faces reality and expects others to do the same.* Effective leaders don't kid themselves. They deal with things the way they really are, not just the way they wish things were. This attitude gives others permission to get real and deny denial as well.

- *Demonstrates faith in people.* Without an attitude of trust, a principal or superintendent can be little more than a policeman constantly on the lookout for violators. ("If you want to get along with people to the best advantage, you must be able to see the good in them rather than the bad."—J. C. Penney)

- *Holds a positive view of the future.* Effective leaders are stubborn in their commitment to hope. ("I dwell in Possibility."—Emily Dickinson) Their realism keeps them from having a Pollyanna attitude, but they steadfastly believe that all obstacles can and will be overcome in the end. It is similar to the "survivor attitude" held by those who endured the holocaust.

- *Shows an open attitude toward change.* Level 5 leaders are willing to shake things up, raise the roof, and turn the organization upside down if necessary to get desired results.

- *Values honesty.* Effective leaders are authentic leaders. Anything less doesn't work, because kids, teachers, parents, and school-board members have a built-in radar for detecting phonies;

- *Reflects an attitude of unselfishness.* You can't be your best as a school leader until you learn to "de-center" yourself—accept that you are not the center of the universe, or even of your own school;

• *Practices humility (without bragging about it).* Effective leaders promise answers and deliver answers, but they don't pretend to have all the answers.

• *Makes it clear that giving up is not an option.* Winston Churchill's "We'll never quit" attitude saved an entire nation in wartime. Just think what it can do for your school.

• *Shows a willingness to accept conflict as part of doing business in a public institution.* Real leaders don't back down from necessary confrontation and aren't afraid of a fight—and everyone knows it. ("Military history is full of generals who don't want to fight. They're called losers."—James Carville, political adviser to presidents)

• *Is passionate about the work and not afraid to show it.* More than anything else, strong emotion—a passion that won't let up—separates peak performers from also-rans. It's true in all organizations and especially true in schools.

To the very best administrators, being a principal or superintendent is more than a job. It is almost a calling. These are the leaders who care for and run their organization as if they owned it. They don't just work *in* the school, they constantly work *on* the school to make it better.

These are most of the distinguishing attitudes that characterize the kind of leaders everyone admires and remembers. But in schools, there is one more. Patience! It deserves separate billing and may well be the most important attitude of all.

School leaders everywhere work in a state of perpetual partial fulfillment. (More than leaders in business, industry, or the military where things get resolved quickly and everyone knows the results.) That's why no school administrator can succeed without a high level of "ambiguity tolerance"—the ability to live with unsolved problems. You and I call it plain, old-fashioned patience.

Scientists frequently talk about "Brownian motion," the irregular movement of microscopic particles suspended in fluid. These particles zig, zag, dip, dive, and constantly move in a random, erratic, patternless manner. That's the way things often happen in schools, too.

The unknown author who wrote the following could have been thinking about your school (or any school):

The world is inundated with disruption; unforeseen dangers; unanticipated opportunities; unmet expectations; alarming new statistics; startling twists of fate; shocking innovations; unheralded improvements; unrealistic requirements; overwhelming demands; contradictory directions; staggering liabilities; astonishing results; sudden strokes of luck; and more.

Sound familiar? It should. It takes an attitude of extreme patience to remain creative and productive in the environment of chronic chaos called school

Closure comes slowly (if at all) to educators, because outcomes are difficult to measure, results are not known for years (if ever), and problems constantly recycle themselves. How many times have you dealt with the same issues over and over again?

Cynics say education just goes around and around in circles. The faithful choose to believe that we simply make progress along an upward spiral.

Either way, if you are going to make it as a school leader, you have to accept ambiguity as the norm, learn to thrive on it, and continually create your own clarity. With the right attitude, a little ambiguity can even be a good thing.

Look over the discussion of Level 5 attitudes one more time. Whenever you find this combination of attitudes in any leader, you've got a keeper. Fortunately, there are many such leaders in our schools today. More than most people realize. You know some of them. You may even be one of them. If not, you can be.

When it comes to leadership, attitudes make all the difference between success or failure, whether you are running a giant corporation or an elementary school. After all, you are your attitudes. They set you apart and help define who you are, what you stand for, how you treat people, and how you get things done. They are the engines that drive your actions.

More important, attitudes are contagious. Everyone in the school (students, staff members, and others) take their cue from the top. As the leader, your attitude either nourishes the organization or poisons it.

Never underestimate the power of your attitudes. If you have any lingering doubts about its importance or don't want to accept this author's word for it alone, read what others have to say:

For success, attitude is equally as important as ability.

—Harry F. Banks

Nothing can stop the man with the right attitude from reaching his goal, nothing on earth can help the man with the wrong attitude.

—W. W. Ziege

Attitude is more important than aptitude.

—William James

There is very little difference in people. But that little difference makes a big difference. The little difference is attitude. The big difference is whether it is positive or negative.

—Clement Stone

Attitude is more important than the past, than education, than money, than circumstances, than what people do or say. It is more important than appearance, giftedness or skills.

—Charles Swindoll

Enough said. Point made. Case closed.

It's conclusive. Attitudes count. But are they enough? Of course not. Otherwise, this book would end right here. Attitudes are meaningful only if they are acted upon. Anyone can talk the right attitudes, but without follow-through, they are only meaningless clichés and empty promises.

The real "good-to-great" leaders in schools, businesses, or anywhere else actually live their attitudes. It is the only way to establish credibility and model their expectations for the organization.

If you wonder how this works in the real world, here are a dozen examples of attention-grabbing actions that reflect the positive attitudes of the school's leader. (Unlike much of what you see on reality TV, it's OK to try these at home.)

1. Establish an open-door, "no-appointment time" before and after school. (Accessibility is an attitude in itself.)

2. Give everyone on staff their own business cards—including clerks, custodians, and bus drivers. It's another way to honor everyone's importance to the organization.

3. Shrink the school's policy manual and make life easier for everyone. In the business world, Nordstrom gets by with just two simple employee policies: Rule #1—Use your good judgment in all situations; and Rule #2—There will be no additional rules. Surely, a mere department store isn't better run than your school.

4. Take out the chairs and hold stand-up faculty meetings. It shortens meeting time, limits posturing and pontificating, and shows respect for everyone's time.

5. Encourage staff members to "blow the whistle" on colleagues for doing a good deed. Then highlight these random acts of kindness on a special bulletin board in the faculty lounge.

6. Hold autopsies, postmortems, and formal funerals for bad ideas tried and failed. (Cam-Corp Industries has used a Screw-Up Box, so that no foul-up goes unnoticed.)

7. Invite selected business and civic leaders to be "Principal for a Day" in your school. There's no better way to demonstrate openness and give important community members an eye-opening idea of what real live principals do every day. It works for the St. Paul (Minnesota) Schools and it can work for you as well.

8. Even in periods of retrenchment, allocate a little money to fund "enhancements" (limited improvements or new programs or services). Especially in dark times, people need to know that the leader is confident for the long haul. No school is ever too poor to invest in getting better.

9. Require teachers and other staff members to bring back and try at least one "crazy idea" from each conference or convention they attend.

10. Start writing "Asking Memos" instead of just "Telling Memos." Confident leaders are never too proud to ask for help and opinions from others.

11. Make it a point to celebrate successes—great or small. Some companies shoot off a cannon. Ringing a bell might be more appropriate for a school.

12. Introduce a "Pay It Forward" week in your school (inspired by the movie of the same name) when students do good deeds for others in advance, instead of waiting to pay back when nice things are done for them.

Of course, you don't have to like any of these suggestions. You can come up with your own. Just follow your attitudes and see where they take you. The bottom line is that your attitudes are your filters for screening behavior options.

If you are not the school leader you want to be or if things aren't going right in your career, look first to your attitude. It's never too late to conduct your own "Attitude Audit."

Don't let a bad attitude get in the way of your success. Bad attitudes lead to bad choices whose negative consequences only give you a bad attitude. It's a cycle of self-imposed frustration and failure. It doesn't have to be that way.

The great thing about attitudes is that you can change them. ("The greatest discovery of my generation is that human beings can alter their lives by altering their attitude of mind."—William James)

Your attitudes are not like DNA. They are not permanently imprinted. You can choose your attitudes and make them work for you instead of against you.

There are lots of factors that make up an effective leader in today's schools. But attitudes come first.

If you don't get anything else out of this section, remember this: There is no good leader with a bad attitude!

B Built-in Backbone

"To fight a bull when you are not scared is nothing," says a well-known bull-fighter, "and not to fight a bull when you are scared is nothing. But to fight a bull when you are scared—that is something."

—Von Dech
writer

If you don't think it takes more backbone than ever before to run a school in America today, you're not paying attention or not doing your job. It may not be the same level of bravery or bravado as needed to face a firing squad, but it's courage nonetheless.

It takes backbone to close a school, change an attendance boundary, take a chance on an inexperienced teacher, discipline a popular coach, turn down a higher paying job because you have unfinished business where you are, tell the school board what they don't want to hear, intervene with an employee who has a drinking problem, tell parents their kid is a jerk, make unpopular decisions, stand up to the union, fire a tenured teacher, expel a student, confront a gang member, buck the system, or try out a weird idea. It takes guts to do all the right things. But that's exactly what effective school leaders have to do every day.

It's not just in large schools or inner-city schools. Leaders of small schools—even rural schools—need extra backbone today.

A good example is the teacher from Piper, Kansas, who resigned because the school board wouldn't back her decision to fail several students for plagiarizing their term project. That took backbone. Her principal also quit. He had his share of backbone, too. Sometimes courage is contagious.

It shouldn't come as a revelation that fortitude is a factor in effective school leadership. A strong backbone has always been an essential part of the anatomy of leaders in all fields.

We all know that military leaders are recognized and rewarded for their bravery. After all, courage is the currency of their craft.

Likewise, business leaders, such as the infamous "Neutron" Jack Welch (former chief executive officer of General Electric) are widely respected for their toughness. Welch became a legend for his gutsy business practices (e.g., increasing spending while downsizing at the same time and rigorously sloughing off nonperformers). Business people like that kind of courage.

Educators do, too. We just don't talk about it much, because we like to think we have a more genteel, compassionate profession. It's not always true. What successful administrators know that mediocre managers often miss is that school leaders and business leaders have a lot in common.

Education is a tough occupation, too. We expect and respect backbone in our leaders as much as anyone. That's why when fellow administrators say a female counterpart "has the balls for the job," they may have the anatomy wrong, but it's intended as a compliment. They just mean she has sufficient backbone to be an effective school leader today.

Every school, every business, every organization wants a leader with built-in backbone. Unfortunately, the demand exceeds the supply. There isn't always enough courage to go around. We all know schools in which the leadership seems to suffer from an acute "courage deficit."

Of course, it's easy to be brave when others aren't depending on you and you don't have responsibility for the welfare of the entire organization. It's a lot more difficult at the top where the wind blows from all directions. ("Boldness becomes rarer the higher the rank."—Karl von Clauswitz)

Spinelessness among leaders can be the result of experiencing too much success too soon, or merely be an example of the "Peter Principle" (being promoted beyond your level of competence). Sometimes, it's just caused by sticking around too long.

Just as osteoporosis can soften the bones with age, the comforts and perks accompanying success and authority can eventually weaken a leader's backbone. It's easy to feel that you have too much to lose to take risks anymore. Some leaders mellow with age, experience, and success. Others "marshmellow."

Cowardice comes in many forms. I remember an elementary school principal who habitually hid behind his office door whenever an irate parent showed up. Another cowered on the floor in the backseat of his car in the parking lot when the pressures of the job became too great. You may know similar situations. Fortunately, these are extreme cases.

Most of the time, cowardly tendencies are more subtle. Often they are just a matter of constantly settling for the easy, popular, comfortable, safe, or politically correct choice—even if it isn't in the best interests of kids. When administrators don't have the stomach to face hard facts and make tough decisions, they are no longer viable leaders of the school. They are merely keeping the seat warm until a real leader comes along.

In today's environment, you cannot be an effective leader of the school—any school—without a strong backbone. Period. And it's only going to be more true tomorrow.

This doesn't mean that you have to be the bravest warrior on the battlefield (*cojones* come in many sizes), but you do have to have the stomach to play for high stakes, possess the inner strength to make hard calls, and be willing to stand up for what's right.

Demonstrating courage on the job as a principal or superintendent doesn't mean slaying dragons. But it does mean you have to do what has to be done—every day! It means doing all you have to do and all you can do to educate all children. It means being willing to act or make decisions just because you are the leader. It means taking responsibility for your acts without hiding behind a spin doctor or engaging in "blamestorming" (seeking creative excuses or pointing fingers for failure).

Bold leadership is what every community wants, what every child deserves, and what every school must have to survive and succeed anymore. If you don't have the backbone to lead this way, you're in the wrong business.

The good news is that none of these components of courage suggest you can't be afraid. Having backbone doesn't mean being fearless. The phrase "fearless leader," is a misnomer.

Effective principals and superintendents aren't brave because they have no fear of failure, criticism, unpopularity, embarrassment, censure, or even possible unemployment. They fear all these things but do the job anyway. ("Courage is knowing you are afraid and doing what needs to be done anyway."—Former New York City mayor, Rudolf Giuliani)

Courage is the will to act in spite of fear. The school leaders you know who have the most backbone still have plenty of fears. What distinguishes them is that they know their fears. They face their fears. But they refuse to be motivated by their fears. Musician-songwriter Kenny Loggins had it right: "Who fears less, leads."

Fortunately, it's OK for school leaders to be afraid. But unfortunately, it's also easy to become afraid in this profession, because there are a lot of people and things to be scared of, including:

Punitive legislatures	Out-of-control kids
Angry taxpayers	Out-of-control parents
Militant teachers	Angry people
Dissatisfied parents	Crazy people
Flakey school board members	… and more
Scheming lawyers	

Naturally, when you are aware of all the dangers, it is awfully tempting to play it safe. Safety is over-rated. Besides, it's a myth:

Who can hope to be safe? Who sufficiently cautious? Guard himself as he may, every moment's an ambush.

—Horace

School leaders can run. And they can hide. But they can never be entirely safe.

Your school and mine have no use for runners and hiders. What's needed are calculated risk takers—leaders with enough backbone to take a chance on doing what's needed, even if it is awkward, inconvenient, uncomfortable, painful, or worse.

Schools are not places for the faint of heart. We don't need more leaders in search of safety.

—Leonard O. Pellicer

Some administrators spend too much time worrying about what business writer Michael Grinder calls HNTGS (How Not To Get Shot) and not enough time worrying about how to give it their best shot every day.

Playing it safe limits choices and lessens your chances of success. Taking risks emboldens you and others and energizes the entire organization. That's what leadership is all about.

Actor Paul Newman once explained his outspoken positions on controversial political issues by saying, "You have to show your ass. You just can't walk in and play it safe." Newman was right. He probably would have made a good principal or superintendent.

Of course, no one can be courageous all the time. That's why savvy leaders choose their battles carefully and ration their bravery accordingly. Timing is everything.

Survival is often a matter of being strong when it counts and caving in when it's inconsequential. The best advice for all school leaders is don't exhaust your fortitude on trifles. And don't draw a line in the sand during a sandstorm.

It also helps to know that courage doesn't have to be larger than life. Sometimes, it is couched in small acts of bravery that go unnoticed. Just showing up can be an act of heroism in the right circumstances.

Whatever our circumstances, most of us are like the cowardly lion in *The Wizard of Oz*. We are not born with courage. We have to go out and find it on our own. We have to grow our own backbone.

How do people do that? Most often, slowly. Incrementally. Like a muscle, backbone grows stronger with use.

Fortunately, there are many building blocks—great and small—that you (or anyone) can use to develop greater courage and to demonstrate that courage to others who need to see it in their leader. Following are a few of the steps that can make you a braver, bolder decision maker:

- *Resist too much comfort.* A cushy office, fancy furnishings, a proliferation of assistants, a paid membership in a health club, a complimentary car, and a VIP parking space don't make it easier to rock the boat. Too much comfort can make cowards of us all.

Resist too many perks and too much pampering based on your title. Avoid hanging out only with the people who always agree with you and make you feel comfortable and safe. Keep it simple. And keep it spartan. That makes it easier to make difficult (and unpopular) decisions when necessary.

- *Draw strength from others.* Courage can be multiplied by a support system (at home and on the job). Network with advisors, supporters, and cheerleaders—both in and out of your field. Business executives often make good mentors for school leaders. It's always easier to get back in the ring when you have a lot of people in your corner.

- *Know your enemies and make the first move.* Learn all you can about the opposition. Knowledge is power. The more you know, the braver you can be. It enables you to be proactive. That puts you in control, and that's where a lot of courage comes from.

- *Reduce your dependencies* (on people, chemicals, or bad habits). The freer you are, the braver you can be. It works every time.

- *Don't always ask permission.* Sometimes, it's easier to be brave when you act first and apologize later.

- *Always have a Plan B.* Being bold goes better when you have a fallback position.

- *Tell the truth.* That way you don't have to remember your lies, and you have one less thing to fear—discovery. Honesty promotes courage.

- *Psyche yourself up.* There's a reason karate pupils shout before they go into competition or combat. The yell (called "kia") raises their adrenalin, increases their strength, and throws their opponents off guard. It also gives them courage. Try yelling or whatever does the job for you. If getting psyched up works in the martial arts, it can work for real-world battles as well.

- *Trust your instincts.* Rely on your intuition to sense danger and signal when you need to stiffen your backbone. In Las Vegas, casino surveillance personnel use the criteria, "JDLR" (Just Don't Look Right) to determine when to act on their suspicions. Your hunches can work the same way for you and can be your best early-warning system.

- *Develop a thick hide.* You will always have critics. Learn not to take them personally. Slough off unwarranted criticism, learn from constructive criticism, and put the rest in perspective. ("All of us could take a lesson from the weather. It pays no attention to criticism."—North DeKalb)

- *Reward risk taking more than you punish failure.* Strive to build a culture in your school that values risk-taking. Once it gets started, it can snowball. Courage begets courage.

- *Demonstrate courage by making yourself vulnerable.* Try exposing yourself to opportunities for students, staff members, and citizens to raise issues that bother them (e.g., favoritism, being left out, what needs more time, where greater support is needed, etc.).

In their best-selling book, *Finding and Keeping Great Employees*, Jim Harris and Joan Brannick even suggest establishing an Internet site (e.g., "tickedoff.com") for upset employees. You have teachers who would love to visit this site.

The more often you face risky situations, the easier it gets. Part of courage is just getting used to what scares you.

- *Make it a habit to do things that make you uncomfortable.* Ride a rollercoaster. Volunteer to give a speech. Surprise yourself by taking some chances and proving to yourself that you can still be a hero. Once you discover that you can be terrified, liberated, and exhilarated all at the same time, you will appreciate courage a lot more.

- *Stay healthy and stay fit.* The better you feel physically, the braver you can be.

- *If nothing else works, fake it.* ("Pretending to be courageous is as good as the real thing."—David Letterman, following September 11, 2001)

- *Have an exit card.* Nothing makes you braver than having someplace else to go.

If none of these suggestions suits you, anything else you can do to get out of your comfort zone will help build backbone. Just simplifying your organizational chart can boost your odds of behaving bravely. Bureaucracies coddle cowards.

Leaders in all fields have to be lots of things. Most of all, they have to be brave enough to do the job the way it should be done. ("Only the bold get to the top."—Publilius Syrus) Fortunately, acting bravely can become a habit. Better yet, it is always rewarded.

In retrospect, many retired administrators agree that, given a choice between courage and smarts, they would now pick courage every time. Most of the regrets harbored by former school leaders stem from lapses in fortitude—incidents in which they failed to stand up soon enough, long enough, or strong enough for what is right.

You can be lots of things in this world without any noticeable degree of courage. Being a principal or superintendent in today's schools isn't one of them. So if you don't have the backbone to lead, at least have the courage to get out of the way.

C Coaching, Culture, and Common Sense

Our culture is our competitive edge.

—Mike Smith
Lands' End

Management is about organized commonsense.

—Andy Grove, president
Intel Corporation

You can't pick up a book on leadership anymore without reading a lot about "coaching" and "culture." (This book is no exception.) Most don't say much about "common sense." ("When last I checked, common sense wasn't a priority." —Michael Ayers)

It's peculiar; because the three go together. And every bona fide leader knows it. To be effective today, leaders, especially school leaders

- Do a lot more coaching than commanding and controlling.
- Recognize the importance of relationships and "chemistry" more than ever and intentionally nurture the internal community (culture) of the organization, instead of just letting it happen.
- Balance vision, enthusiasm, and ambition with realism, reasonableness, and good sense.

If that doesn't sound exactly like the way you run your school, you may be missing a few good bets. None of us is perfect, but we can all get better. That's what books on leadership are for.

The principals and superintendents who really "get it" understand that coaching is the cornerstone of effective leadership. This means that old roles, such as directing, policing, and enforcing, have to be replaced with new functions, including teaching, counseling, influencing, inspiring, facilitating, and prospecting for resources.

The best school leaders today have learned to accept not being totally in control and are willing to give away power. You can learn this, too.

We all know that good coaches listen, probe, and help others find solutions on their own. They provide emotional support and allow others to grow. So what else is new? This is what lasting leaders have done all along.

Without the burden of having to know all the answers and being in complete control, leaders are free to look for, and actually admit and correct, weak spots and problems in the making (e.g., boredom, cynicism, bottlenecks, road blocks, paper pileups, and people with not enough to do—or too much to do).

There's a reason that successful coaches painstakingly review past performances, develop a whole play book of alternatives and options, build on strengths, and encourage team members to practice what works. It's called winning. When school leaders behave as coaches, it creates a whole different—and better—culture within the organization. Schools can be winners, too.

Every organization has its own distinctive culture that largely determines how people act and react. You are the type of leader you are, in part, because of the culture to which you've been exposed.

Even the culture of different countries produces different types of leadership styles. In Asian cultures, managers stress group (team) success over individual accomplishment. In Scandinavia, leaders are expected to nurture employees, not push them. In many strict Muslim nations, if you're a leader, you're male. Female managers aren't allowed. It's all in the culture.

Likewise, the culture of your school defines how teachers teach, how kids learn, how people get along together (or don't), and how much success you'll have. Culture is powerful. But what is it?

The culture of an organization is simply its inner reality (socially transmitted behavior, assumptions, and patterns) that shapes how people behave and interact. It is perpetuated through ceremonies, celebrations, rituals, stories, heroes, habits, and traditions.

Most schools (like any other organization) have both an overt culture (how the policy manual say things are done) and a covert culture (how things are really done).

The anatomy of your school's culture includes the following:

- *Purposes.* Why the organization exists. Its core idea. Why people get out of bed and come to work every day.
- *Values.* What the organization believes, what it stands for. Its norms (unwritten rules). What's recognized. Rewarded. Encouraged. Allowed. Preferred. What's important. What's out of bounds. How people treat each other. What's safe. And what's not.
- *Image.* The organization's picture of the future. Its vision. How it plans to win. How it will know when it does.
- *Goals.* What needs to be done. The steps to be taken. The benchmarks.
- *Roles.* Who does what. Who has the power. And why.
- *Systems.* Strategies. Rules. Support systems. Policies. Procedures. Rewards. Penalties.

When you add all this up, you have the true character of the organization. Writer William Bridges may explain it best: "Character is the personality of the organization; it is the DNA of the organizational life form. It is the organization's character that makes it feel and act like itself."

Naturally, there are all kinds of cultures. Some are better, stronger, healthier, and more successful than others. In *Finding and Keeping Great Employees,* Jim Harris and Joan Brannick identify four core business cultures:

1. *Customer service cultures:* organized to create customer satisfaction.

2. *Innovative cultures:* organized to create the future.

3. *Operational excellence cultures:* organized to constantly improve productivity and efficiency and reduce costs.

4. *Spirit cultures:* organized to create an environment that inspires personal excellence.

Does your school fit into any of these categories? If not, my favorite way to sort out cultures is simply the following:

1. Every man for himself

2. Us versus them

3. Superficial teaming and camaraderie

4. Culture of caring

Your school must fit in there somewhere.

Regardless of category, the scary part is that the kind of culture your school has is mostly your fault—or to your credit. More than anything else, cultures are the creations of leaders.

Contrary to what many people think, culture isn't the function of geography, demographics, economics, or even size (e.g., it is possible for a corporation to downsize and merely end up with a smaller bureaucracy consisting of fewer layers but the same strictures and restrictions). Culture is a function of leadership.

No one can completely script a culture, but it doesn't happen all by itself either. In your school, you strongly influence the culture

- By what you say. When you tell people what you want and expect, most will believe you. Many will try to give it to you.

- By what you model. People believe what you do even more than what you say. The culture of most organizations reflects the behavior of their respective leaders.

- By what you pay attention to. One of the greatest gifts any leader can give is "attention." ("When attention is not paid to nurturing shared assumptions of high expectations, the shared assumptions fall to the lowest common denominator. Schools become organized around dysfunctional norms and the routines, policies, even architectural features, build up to support the way things have always been done."—Jill Harrison Ray)

- By what you recognize and reinforce. You get what you reward.

Whether you like it or not, if you are a principal or superintendent, you're a culture builder. That's why it pays to be intentional about it and to do it right.

A great culture makes a great organization. Businesses recognize this. Schools should, too. ("The relationships we have with our people and the culture of our company is our most sustainable competitive edge."—Howard Schultz, founder, Starbucks)

Your school's culture can be your leg up on the competition. (Yes, you are competing whether you admit it or not. Your competition includes charter schools, magnet schools, other public schools, private and parochial schools, and the growing popularity of home schooling.)

A positive culture attracts champions. Great teachers can teach anywhere. There is never a shortage of jobs for top talent. Consequently, the best teachers gravitate to schools where they connect with the culture. You want that to be your school.

So what kind of culture do you want to develop within your organization? Here's what I want in any school with which I'm associated (see if you agree).

Think of the best possible learning environment for kids that you can imagine. A school where every child is known and cared about; where excellence is prized, hard work is recognized, and fun is a priority; where students pull for each other and take care of each other; where something interesting and exciting is happening all the time and everyone wants to show up every day.

Where everyone's contribution is appreciated and no one falls through the cracks; where everyone feels they belong; where people want to do their best because everyone else is; where being different is OK and being yourself is mandatory; where people can try, fail, try harder, fail better, and eventually succeed; where information is freely shared and problems are squarely faced.

Where success is assumed because it always happens sooner or later; where people are positive, hopeful, and optimistic; where people compete and cooperate with equal intensity; where encouragement and support are givens; and where expectations are realistic, rules are reasonable, and common sense is contagious.

Now replicate that kind of environment for grown-ups. Voila! You have a winning school culture. What works for kids works for adults. It's that simple. What makes a great place for children to study and learn makes a great place for adults to teach and work as well.

I recently heard about the Connec Time p.m. Cyber Café at the Southview Middle School in Edina, Minnesota. Located next to the school's media center, the "café," which is open until 8 p.m. two nights a week, is just a comfortable place for students to hang out and do their homework.

In addition to providing open access to computers so kids can surf the Internet, the setting features conversational arrangements of comfy chairs and couches. They even sell drinks (smoothies) and have open-mike sessions for kids to tell jokes and have poetry slams. What kid wouldn't like such a setup? What adult wouldn't as well?

The point is that any school that interesting and that interested in its students has got to be a welcoming, exciting, and satisfying place for teachers, clerks, cooks, custodians, and other adults, too. That's the way school cultures work.

Going to a job every day in a healthy school culture feels like living in a close-knit community. I've had that feeling. (A few times—not all the time. Surprise! It was always the leader who made the difference.) You probably have had the feeling, too. It's a good thing.

Some administrators even boast that in their school, "We are a family." That may be a little too much to expect from an external organization, but a sense of community is close enough. It's what you want in your school.

Of course, this kind of optimal culture can't descend on any organization overnight. Even powerful business leaders can't mandate a winning culture by fiat, executive order, or public announcement. It has to be built incrementally through careful coaching and the accumulation of small ideas, acts, and shared experiences. How does that work?

Following are some practical suggestions (building blocks) that have contributed to the positive cultures in some of the successful schools and businesses you've heard about. They just might help energize your school culture as well.

• Set aside regular "Good News Days" on which everyone must talk only about the good things going on in the organization.

• Integrate break areas. Do away with the traditional "teachers' lounge" and separate coffee rooms for other employees.

• Allow employees to give each other sick leave or personal leave days to cover emergency situations.

• Promote informal team-building activities (e.g., shooting hoops, darts tournaments, bowling parties, or playing pool).

• Put a new face on failure. Give it a better image. After all, 97 percent of all work ends in some degree of failure. Edison looked on failures as milestones. If it was good enough for an inventive genius, it should be good enough for you. Never make the penalty for failure greater than the penalty for not trying at all in your school.

• Be sure to have some fun. Make laughter, humor, and smiles a daily ritual. The Play Fair Co. in Berkeley, California, has gone so far as to put fake fish in the company water cooler and to staple Kleenex to memos containing bad news. Are you up for those kind of high jinks?

• Start off monthly meetings with the question, "Why do we work here?"

• Set aside VIP parking spots for pregnant employees.

• Designate an in-house poet laureate to write humorous, tongue-in-the-cheek poems to honor employees on special occasions (e.g., birthdays and retirements) or for special achievements. If you don't have a budding poet on staff, an in-house cartoonist can serve the same function.

• Help everyone on your staff see how what they do directly connects to student and school success. It's been a while since Dr. Abraham Maslow observed that workers at the end of the assembly line are always the most productive, because they see the final outcome and have a sense of accomplishment and contribution. His findings still hold true. This applies to school personnel as well as to factory workers.

Teachers see direct results for their efforts. It's more difficult for other personnel. Help them make the connections they don't readily see for themselves.

• Mobilize assistance for employees who experience an emergency or crisis in their life away from the school (e.g., house fire, family death, hospitalization, injury).

• Find ways for your staff to join together to give back to the community. Every school staff counts on community support and should do something to improve the community in return. Possibilities include giving blood; building houses with Habitat for Humanity; walkathons; recycling; adopting a street, highway, or park; or helping with a community garden. You and your staff can think of many more service opportunities. It's even better if you can involve students, too.

• Respect every staff member's time. Don't waste it by giving poor instructions, making them wait, interrupting their work, or keeping them guessing.

• Make sure secretaries and aides get their share of credit and recognition for their bosses' achievements.

• Create a physical environment that reflects your culture. Feng Shui isn't just for homes. Make liberal use of posters and artwork that inspires and sends the right message. Minimize perks in the front office. Spruce up the rest of the facility where the real teaching and learning takes place instead.

• Before a big event, dare to pull your team together, form a huddle, call the play, and end with a cheer. Who says a healthy school culture can't be a little corny now and then?

• Think like a magnet school. Develop what business maven Tom Peters calls a "Wow" factor—a theme, program, event, or style that sets your school apart, allowing individuals on your staff to "step out" and the whole organization to "stand out" from the rest of the look-alikes and cookie-cutter schools. There's an advantage in being unique. It gives every employee something to be proud of.

• Free up teachers any way you can. Freedom is a reward—especially for teachers who don't have much to start with.

• Be sure to thank the spouses and families of employees for their sacrifices and support.

• Play the Smile Game. See how many people you can get to smile back at you during the day. Keep score. See if you can beat your own record. Smiling is contagious, and your school could use an epidemic.

• If you have young parents on your staff, arrange for on-site day care if possible. It's what convinced *Woman's* magazine to name General Mills as one of the top places in the country for mothers to work. Surely your school is as good as any cereal company.

• Initiate an EAP (Employee Assistance Program) to provide employees and their families with confidential assistance for mental and emotional problems, substance abuse or dependencies, and economic or health crises.

• Respect staff members' family time. Don't expect custodians and other employees who are parents to work overtime every time.

• Arrange for someone to pick up and deliver prescriptions for staff members who have trouble getting away during the school day.

• Pull out all the stops. Do whatever works to make your school's culture the place people want to be. Take a tip from Tara Litin, CEO of Litin Paper, who has been known to use "communication, hugs, show tunes, cheerleading, and common sense" to build a winning culture in the family paper business. Can you dare to do any less?

When you add up all of these ideas (along with any other comparable initiatives you may think of), you get a school culture that is greater than the sum of these parts.

As it turns out, there is nothing magic about creating a winning culture or ethos for your school. What it takes most is "instinctive savvy" and common sense. ("Common sense is genius dressed in work clothes." — Ralph Waldo Emerson) And did I mention a lot of hard work? But it's worth it.

Leading a school today is like playing with an old-fashioned Chinese finger trap. You know, the kind where you insert your forefingers and then try to pull them out. The harder you pull in opposite directions, the tighter the trap grips your fingers. The trick is simply to bring your fingers together, and the trap releases.

The lesson of the Chinese finger trap metaphor is that your school can't succeed as long as everyone is pulling in different directions. You're trapped. It succeeds only when people come together. ("Coming together is a beginning, keeping together is progress, working together is success."—Henry Ford) That's where coaching and the culture of the organization come in.

If you are like many principals and superintendents, you don't ordinarily spend much time thinking about the ethos of your organization. Maybe it's time to start.

The truth is that with a "pulling apart" culture, your school will always be mediocre—at best. That's a promise. With a "pull-together" culture, you have a shot at greatness. More than anything else, it's the culture that determines if your school falls short of the standard, meets the standard, or raises the standard every day.

If you only remember one thing from this chapter, make it this: Whenever you see an outstanding school—the kind you want yours to be—its success doesn't lie in the curriculum. It lies in the coaching, the culture, and the leader's common sense. This could be your school!

D Do the Next Right Thing

. . . ethics is simple: if something stinks, don't do it.

—Neal St. Anthony
business columnist

Live in such a way that you would not be ashamed to sell your parrot to the town gossip.

—Will Rogers
American humorist

When you don't know what to do, just do the next right thing.

—AA saying

Oh, No! Not another boring treatise on ethics! Yep. That's what it is. And with no apologies.

If this book were set up on the basis of priorities, rather than being organized in alphabetical order, this would be Chapter 1. It's that important.

You may not want to read more about ethical behavior, but if you are the leader of a school of any size, anywhere, you need to. You can't have too many reminders that ethics is never obsolete—especially in schools.

If you want to be a successful school leader today (even if you want to be only a mediocre one), integrity is the most important leadership trait you can develop.

Despite today's sensational headlines and tabloid tales, the best leaders in all conceivable professions or occupations (except, perhaps, Mafia chiefs and drug dealers) continue to be principle-centered. They live their values (walk the talk) and practice value-based decision making every day.

No leader operates in a vacuum. Decisions have to be based on some guiding principles or values. Egotism, ambition, and personal gain are not valid core values. Decency, fair play, honesty, and truthfulness are. They don't become old-fashioned—or if they do, "It is better to be old-fashioned and right, than to be up-to-date and wrong."—Tiorio.

In our society, schools are expected to be "virtuous enterprises." They are held to a higher standard, and so are their leaders. That includes you.

It may not be fair. It may not be just. It may not even be realistic. But it is a fact. If you can't live with it, now would be a good time to quit reading this book and get one on changing careers.

There are many reasons ethics (doing the next right thing) is especially important for school officials. Here are my personal favorites:

1. *Educational leadership is a sacred trust.* If this sounds like a sermon, it is. A sermon you probably need to hear periodically. I know I do.

Trust is the lifeblood of public education. You can't run your school without it. And the only way to earn trust is to be trustworthy.

Being a school leader may not be a "calling," but it comes close. Only special people can do it right—people with a passion for the highest human values.

After all, children are involved. That means everyone must be treated right. That's what ethics is all about. You don't have to be a saint to be a superintendent or principal. But it doesn't hurt.

2. *It has to start somewhere.* Can you imagine how disillusioned today's students must be? They repeatedly hear of graft and corruption in government, wrongdoing in business, scandals in professional sports, and even abuse in the church. Where do kids (and adults) find role models for moral behavior these days? How about in your school?

Schools don't simply teach young people what's-what and how-to; they teach them what to be and how to be. Educators teach who they are.

If schools don't model ethical, principled behavior, who will? You don't have a choice. If you can't demonstrate to kids and the community what a life of decency looks like, you are not fit to lead a school. No caveats. No comprises. No kidding.

If you think that's too tall an order, tell me how much less you're willing to take in the school leaders who inform, instruct, and inspire your children or grandchildren.

School administrators can't be perfect, but they must constantly try to do the next right thing—not just try a little bit, but try hard every day and never stop trying. It has to start somewhere.

3. *Ethics is contagious.* If a leader sets a high standard of principled behavior, it can permeate the entire organization—any organization. The

leader's example determines how people, at all levels, carry out their duties and treat others. It can start an epidemic of ethics. That's a healthy thing for any organization.

What makes a value-based school that supports tolerance, integrity, and scrupulous honesty? A value-based leader. A principled principal makes a principled school. It's that simple. You can't have a squeaky clean school with a corrupt or morally bankrupt administrator.

4. *People enjoy working in an ethical environment.* They even work harder. Working by a strict code of core values engages the soul of everyone associated with the school. Teachers and other employees who are inspired by a leader's unflinching integrity are more energized, more loyal, and more productive.

You can't cheat, lie, cut corners, or take unfair advantage and expect your staff to feel good about themselves, their job, or their school. People don't do their best when they constantly feel guilty about how the organization operates.

5. *A reputation for high ethical standards is the best possible advertisement.* The best teachers, the best students, and the best families are attracted to a school known for its integrity. So are the lion's share of resources.

In times of open enrollment, school choice, charter schools, alternative schools, parent vouchers, and home schooling, this is not a bad thing.

Obviously, the need for a high level of ethics is as strong (or stronger) in schools as in businesses and other organizations. Fortunately, the incidences of indiscretions are less frequent in schools and the infractions themselves are often more subtle.

Most school administrators don't have the opportunity to "cook the books" and make off with billions in profits like some of their counterparts in business. Their misdeeds are usually less spectacular. Sometimes they even go almost unnoticed.

I'm reminded of the example of a superintendent whose style was to lie, ration, or withhold information according to self-interests; to manipulate people, play favorites, conceal sensitive budget items, and disregard contract provisions when they interfered with personal goals. Most outsiders, not even the school board, ever caught on. None of this behavior constituted criminal misconduct. Or malfeasance. Or perhaps even malpractice. But it was unethical. You don't have to be totally rotten to be less fresh and clean than you should be.

Even a little unprincipled behavior takes its toll on the institution. In this case, the penalty was lower morale, heightened mistrust, and the exodus of several talented administrators who became uncomfortable with the clouded ethical climate within the organization.

Principles are not matters of degree. Like pregnancy, you can't be a little bit ethical. You either are or you aren't.

Some school officials try to defend fluid ethics by claiming that the line of demarcation between right and wrong has become blurred. Hogwash! This is an excuse, not an explanation.

In most situations, the next right thing is fairly obvious. What's often lacking is the will to do it.

If you want to know what's right, look to your professional organization's adopted code of ethics. (Yes, every association of school administrators has one.) Ignorance of the code is no excuse. Leading your school without being familiar with the code of ethics is like trying to do your job without reading the job description.

But even without a formal code of ethics, distinguishing right from wrong is seldom complicated. Some writers suggest simply applying a "smell test." Others propose using your mother as the standard—If you wouldn't want to tell you mom what you're doing, you probably shouldn't be doing it. Former network TV executive Fred Friendly explained it this way: "Can I live with it? If not, don't do it."

Most of us have a fairly accurate moral compass. In the education business, there are many choices to make, but only one standard to apply—what's good for kids. ("Nothing you do for a child is ever wasted."—Garrison Keillor)

Knowing what direction to go isn't usually the problem. Accepting the compass reading and actually following it, when it doesn't point to where we want to go, is what can be difficult.

Of course, school administrators aren't the only leaders faced with tough moral choices and ethical dilemmas. Business executives are, too, and in business, the temptations, opportunities, and stakes are often much greater. We've all read tales of obscene excesses by unscrupulous CEOs.

Yet surprisingly enough, principals and superintendents can still learn a few things about principled leadership from successful CEOs. The ethical lessons and examples from business aren't limited to what not to do.

Believe it or not, the vast majority of corporate executives are still trying to do the right thing. Not necessarily because of their intrinsic purity, but because ethical behavior is good for commerce. In business, as in education, core values are essential to success.

Stephen Covey, prize-winning author, sums it up best:

Principle centered leaders operate on self-evident, self-validating laws (fairness, equity, honesty, trust, integrity). These are the "compasses of the organization."

If you still think business leaders don't take ethics seriously, you haven't heard what Harvey Mackay tells audiences of corporate leaders across the country:

The one pain Tylenol won't cure, however, is the headache that comes from knowing you mishandled a situation by putting money, office, politics or fear ahead of ethics and integrity. . . .

   But if decisions are made from the top down based on solid corporate values, customers know immediately that their confidence is well-placed.

   . . . Our value is the sum of our values.

Wow! No educator could say it any better.

Perhaps the best lesson on ethics that principals and superintendents can learn from the business world is the finding of a 2001 study conducted by the Center of Ethical Business Cultures (maybe the education profession needs a similar watchdog group.)

The center's research unequivocally concluded that business executives who "walk their talk" on ethical leadership and their companies are clearly the best long-term performers.

It's as true for schools as it is for businesses. The ultimate secret to success is simply doing what's right every time, all the time.

Whether it's in a business or a school, principled leadership looks the same. Here's how ethical principals, superintendents, CEOs, and business managers act and what they do regularly and routinely:

• Keep promises, honor commitments. and stick to their word. ("A promise is an IOU."—Robert Half)

• Tell the truth. ("To be persuasive, we must be believable. To be believable, we must be credible. To be credible, we must be truthful."—Edward R. Morrow)

• Are open about their intentions. (No hidden agendas.)

• Say what they mean and mean what they say.

• See what needs to be done and do it without waiting to be asked (or told). ("To see what's right and not do it, is want of courage, or of principle."—Confucius)

• Accept blame.

• Obey laws and rules.

• Avoid half-truths.

- Remain loyal.

- Follow due process.

- Give a full day's work for a full day's pay.

- Strive to be impartial.

- Champion institutional integrity, so that employees feel free—even duty bound—to do the right thing. Good leaders create a working climate in which the truth is heard. They make it known that honesty not only counts, it is an expectation.

- Adhere to the spirit, not just the letter, of their principles. This means not only doing what's right, but fighting for what's right.

- Make the harder right choices, over the easier wrong ones.

- Conduct their off-duty behavior in a manner that promotes a positive public view of the organization's values.

- Stay totally committed to integrity. No wiggling. No waffling. No weaseling. ("You cannot fake it. You must stand up for what's right regardless. You cannot maintain your integrity 90% and be a leader. It's got to be 100%."—Leonard Roberts, CEO Tandy's, parent company of Radio Shack)

- Build in a "red flag" mechanism to signal potential ethical lapses. Principled leaders protect whistle-blowers instead of penalizing or punishing them.

- Promote the greatest good for the greatest number.

- Continually strive to become and remain qualified for the job. ("You have to try to be what you have to be."—Former New York City mayor Rudolf Giuliani)

Of course, listing the behaviors that characterize value-based leadership is easy. Living the list is much harder.

One measure that can bolster your efforts to become a principled leader is to write a personal integrity statement. Victor M. Parachin, well-known minister, journalist, and author, first proposed putting commitment to principles in writing. Subsequently, many leaders in a variety of fields have accepted the challenge. A representative integrity statement is as follows:

Personal Integrity Statement *(Example)*

I, [your name here], pledge to strive continuously to live my life, on and off the job, based on honesty and truthfulness. I dedicate my position as educational leader to the principles of integrity, credibility, and good character and will faithfully model these values in all my affairs. I will not place personal gain above integrity. I will conscientiously try to do the right thing, as I understand it, in all situations.

_____

[Signature]

School leadership is a complex, technical, layered undertaking. But sometimes we make it more complicated than it needs to be. When it comes to integrity, it's really quite simple.

Someone once suggested to me a four-word credo and a one-sentence job description for all school leaders:

School Leadership

Credo: It's not about me.

Duties: My only job is to do the right thing.

That about says it all.

You may not be the smartest administrator in the profession, or the best educated, or the most charismatic. But you can be as honest, upright, forthright, and truthful as the very best in the business. Here's where you can be in the top 1 percent. The only things that can stop you are lack of will or lack of discipline. Don't let them.

With integrity, anything is possible. Without it, nothing is.

When we think of good character, it's hard to find a better role model than Abraham Lincoln. He also just may have given us the best advice of all on principled leadership: "Let us have faith that right makes might, and in that faith let us to the end dare to do our duty as we understand it."

It's pretty hard to improve on Honest Abe.

E Exceeding Expectations

We are all about exceeding expectations . . .

—David Neeleman, founder
jetBlue airlines

I f you've read this far, you realize that there is no single secret to success as a school leader. But there is one surefire way to take a quantum leap toward effective leadership.

If you really want to set yourself and your school apart as recognized leaders, do what all the best businesses, government agencies, nonprofit organizations and other winning schools do—exceed expectations! It's that simple. And it works every time. Sound hard? Not really. Read on.

Exceeding expectations is the earmark of leadership, excellence, and success for individuals and organizations alike. It's true in all fields and at all levels.

If you are like many of your colleagues, however, you may be skeptical. Some school officials think that exceeding expectations may be OK for business organizations but not for schools. They complain that society already expects more of schools than they can deliver. So how can a school, a principal, or a superintendent possibly go beyond what's expected? It's easier than you think.

The beauty of exceeding expectations is that (a) it's doable (most people—including students, parents, taxpayers and school board members—have become so conditioned to so-so service and mediocre performance that it doesn't take much to please and surprise them) and (b) it's contagious (when you exceed expectations for your job, it raises the level of expectation throughout the organization).

If you are still doubtful of the power of exceeding expectations, look around you at the real world in which you live. The best and most successful performers (the leaders) in every line of work and at every rung of the ladder do it. The examples are everywhere:

- The server who remembers preferences, provides refills without being asked, and is willing to figure out separate checks for a party gets bigger tips than a counterpart who merely keeps the orders straight and brings the food as usual.

- The athletes who break records are the ones who do more than what's expected during training and in practice. (It wasn't just a coincidence that Hall of Famers, Joe Dimaggio and Ted Williams took more batting practice than all their teammates combined.)

- The most successful salespersons are always the ones who, at the end of every workday, make one more call than expected. (That's more than 300 more calls a year. No wonder they lead in sales.)

- The businesses (regardless of service or product) that do it right the first time every time and deliver more than expected, sooner than expected, for less than expected, beat their competition every time. Everyone knows who they are (McDonald's, Nordstrom, Disney, Home Depot), just as they know which schools are the ones to beat in your community or state.

- It's not just big companies that surpass expectations. Successful little ones do, too. A classic example is the small, upstart airline jetBlue, which amazed industry observers by turning a profit selling cheap seats in only one and a half years of operation. How did jetBlue do it? By providing delightful and unexpected good customer service, including a free satellite TV at every seat.

The examples of achieving success by surpassing routine expectations are everywhere. But can it really be done in schools? In your school? You bet. It happens every day. It's happening in a classroom or school office near you. Administrators you know and respect work beyond their job description all the time. You can, too.

If you need more convincing, here are five recent real-world illustrations from a single metropolitan area:

1. Most high school students expect to have a good first day of school. But they don't expect to see yard signs all along their school bus route proclaiming, "Our Kids Come First" or to be greeted at the school entrances by dozens of adult volunteers wishing them well.

Likewise, they don't expect to have only an abbreviated class schedule and then be guests at an outdoor barbeque, complete with games, contests, entertainment, and other surprises hosted by more community volunteers.

None of this is what students normally count on. But this kind of "Day One" program is the way a number of Twin City schools now kick off each new school year. That's exceeding expectations.

2. Teachers usually expect to be appreciated and well received by administrators when they return to school each fall. But they don't expect the principal and his family to decorate each classroom personally with handmade welcome-back mobiles. That's an exceptional expression of appreciation that's unlikely to be forgotten. That's exactly why Fran Crisman, principal of St. Louis Park Junior High, did it.

3. People expect their superintendent to be visible. But they don't expect to see the superintendent handing out programs at concerts and other school events. Nevertheless, Carol Johnson, superintendent of the Minneapolis Public Schools, has been known to do it. When she does, parents notice. So do kids. That's going above and beyond expectations. Maybe that's one reason Dr. Johnson is one of the most sought-after school leaders in the nation.

4. Communities expect school leaders to put marginal students on probation. But they don't expect the superintendent to put whole schools on probation for subpar performance. Yet that's exactly what Pat Harvey, who heads the St. Paul schools, has done. By overreaching normal expectations, Dr. Harvey has earned unprecedented support from business leaders and community members.

5. Citizens and taxpayers expect their schools to be accountable. But they don't expect their schools to "guarantee satisfaction." What school system would promise any patron, dissatisfied with his or her education upon graduation, an opportunity to return for additional help, tutoring, or class work at no cost? The Wayzata (Minnesota) schools did it. No wonder they are recognized as one of the leading school districts in the state. Would you risk such a guarantee? If not, it might be time to ask "why not?"

Get the idea? The lesson is clear. In every existing job category and in every conceivable type of organization, doing more than what is expected is the mark of the real leaders. Schools are no exception.

You can ignore the lesson if you like, but the peers and mentors you look up to take it seriously.

As the head of your schools, if you show up, follow the rules, do what's required, and fulfill all the duties in your position description, that's good management. But it's not leadership. Leaders always do a little bit more.

Surpassing what clients or customers or students or teachers or parents or school boards assume you will do always pays off. It works as well in schools as in businesses. And it works without fail.

There's a reason that Perot Systems, Inc. boasts that its work style is to "do what we say we are going to do and even more." Perot wants to be the leader in its field. And that's the way to do it.

When you and your school "wow" people with unusual and unexpected work or service, you get noticed, admired, and emulated. Your performance level becomes the standard others shoot for. People naturally follow school leaders who perform above the average and beyond the ordinary. That could be you.

Doing enough to get through the day, every day, is OK. It's what most people (including many school administrators) do. But it won't make you a leader. The best principals and superintendents in the business realize that success comes from surprising people (sometimes even yourself) by doing more than is requested or required.

This doesn't mean that leadership is simply a matter of working longer and harder or just doing more of the same thing that everybody else does. That's workaholism. Not leadership.

Neither is leadership a function of excessive busyness. Unfortunately, some wannabe school leaders mistake activity for accomplishment. We've all known colleagues who suffer from "Rocking Chair Syndrome"—They engage in lots of motion; but they don't go anywhere. It's hard for people to follow a stationary object.

The trick is to give a better, more distinctive performance than most people bargained for. Even a little something extra can make a big difference.

If you really want to cross the bridge from routine management to respected leadership, find ways to give your students, parents, staff members, bosses, and community more than they expect. You may be astounded by the results and surprised by how little extra it takes to distance a leader from the pretenders and the also-rans.

If you are interested, there are lots of ways for schools and school leaders to exceed expectations. Only you know what you and your school are capable of and what you are willing to risk. To help prime the pump of possibilities, following are more simple suggestions to get you started:

- When staff members do something really outstanding, don't just praise them. Tell their parents about it. No employee would ever expect that. Make parents proud, and you'll have a loyal follower for life.

- Take your cell phone along whenever you are Managing While Walking Around (MWWA). As you move throughout the school, use it to call parents with positive news about their children. Whoever heard of a principal or superintendent calling a parent with *Good* News? You will be amazed by how much good will can be generated by a few simple phone calls.

- To keep your vision fresh in everyone's mind, put your mission statement and key goals inside fortune cookies and hand them out to staff members. It caught employees' attention when the Intel Corporation tried it. And it can work with your school staff as well.

- Go out in the neighborhoods and talk to representative parents about what they expect of a school leader. In turn, dare to share what you expect from parents. That's probably never been done in your community before.

- Make it a rule in your office that whenever the phone rings, everyone rushes to be the first to answer it. Callers will be bowled over when they actually get to talk to a real human being after only a few rings—and without ever being put on hold or having to listen to an annoying menu of recorded options. You can't buy better public relations than that.

- Try allowing some of your nonteaching personnel to set their own work schedules. It reduced absenteeism by 30 percent at Xerox. Why not in your school?

- Answer your own phone. Make home visits. Send handwritten notes. Students and parents aren't accustomed to that level of attention. That's the whole point of exceeding expectations.

Of course, these examples are only teasers (the basis for a beginning). Undoubtedly, you can think of many more and better ways to exceed expectations that suit your own situation.

None of the suggestions are earthshaking or expensive. But each one can make an impression and make a difference. They are the kinds of small acts that can set you and your school apart. They go beyond what people normally experience. That's the way effective leaders operate.

If you decide to get serious about exceeding expectations, a good way to start is to make it a regular habit to do something out of your comfort zone—something that scares you a little or something that others are not willing to do. Make doing something unusual a routine part of your life. It boosts self-confidence and increases your tolerance for stretching and risk taking.

Once you get used to surprising yourself (exceeding your own expectations for yourself), you are more prepared to start surprising others by doing the exceptional and the unexpected.

People in all fields and professions tend to live up or down to what is expected of them. If you expect the best from yourself and others in the school, you will usually get it. When the leader expects all members of the organization to work toward becoming their best, most of them will.

This is the only surefire way to transcend the inertia of mediocrity. Exceeding expectations can become the norm in any organization, including your school. But only leaders—superintendents, principals, assistant principals, supervisors, and department heads—can make it happen.

Complex organizations (your school is one of them) either grow—get better, not necessarily bigger—lie dormant, or die. All successful organizations have to outdo themselves continually. They do this by consistently exceeding expectations—their own and everyone else's. This raises the bar permanently, for themselves and others at the same time.

If you want to be an effective leader in today's schools, simply do what you do better than people expect you to do it. The best leaders in any field routinely redefine the possible by causing the exceptional to become the ordinary.

It sounds hard. But it seems difficult only because most school officials never try. The school leaders you admire most actually do it. You can, too. If you do, you may just surprise yourself, amaze your supporters, confound your critics, and make your mother proud.

F Fun and the Fish Market Philosophy

Work made fun gets done.

> —Stephen C. Lundin, Harry Paul,
> and John Christensen, authors
> *FISH*

Have fun. If you're not, find out why not and change it.

> —One of the Pride Principles
> adopted by USAA Insurance Company

If you create a place known for laughter, guess what? Cheerful people want to work there. Laughter is an employee benefit.

> —Dale Dauten
> syndicated columnist

How many times have you heard administrators who are about to retire or who wish they could retire say, "It's not fun anymore"? They don't realize what a damning declaration that is.

When the leader of the school isn't having any fun, the teachers probably aren't either—and neither are the kids. What kind of school is that?

When done right, there is joy in learning, and excitement—and fun. If it's not working that way in your school, something is broken. And it's your job to fix it!

Teachers know that students do better when they are having fun. Why don't all principals and superintendents understand that the same principle applies to adults (teachers and other staff members) as well?

Healthy organizations have fun. It's an easy lesson to forget. Don't.

If you ever need a powerful reminder, check out the 2000 blockbuster business best-seller *FISH: A Remarkable Way to Boost Morale and Improve Results* by Stephen C. Lundin, Harry Paul, and John Christensen. According to these authors, fishmongers in Seattle's Pike Place Market work at a hard, dirty, smelly job—and have a good time doing it. Their antics and good humor are legendary. Throwing fish around, yelling jibes at each other and kidding with customers are part of their everyday routine. Obviously, they enjoy their work. And, most important, they sell a whale of a lot of fish.

There's a message in the "fish philosophy" for all leaders. If the fun-filled, bustling, joyful atmosphere of controlled madness gets remarkable results at the fish market, why wouldn't it work in other organizations? In businesses? In schools?

It would. It does every day. Just look at the best school you know. Are the people there having fun learning and working? You know the answer. Fun works.

There's a reason that nationally recognized employers such as Target or Barnes & Noble have hired Chart House International Learning (an organizational training firm in Burnsville, Minnesota) to run "fish camps" designed to teach the fish philosophy, promote fun at work, and legitimatize the power of play on the job.

"Fish" is a motivational attitude and philosophy. ("It's about a new way to work."—John Christensen, Chart House CEO)

As taught at the "fish camps," the lessons of the fish market are bound into four simple principles:

1. *Play.* It's not just something for after work. It's what gets people out of bed and on the job each morning. And it's what makes work more than just getting through the day.

It's not just the families who play together who stay together. It's entire organizations. It's a thriving fish market. Or a good school. Maybe yours.

2. *"Be there" in the moment.* Having fun requires paying attention, not just cruising on autopilot. It pays to notice what's going on. What bloopers occur? What's funny? What's ridiculous? And laugh about it.

Making the most of the lighter side of education is one of those success secrets people are always talking about.

3. *Choose a positive attitude.* It's all about attitude. And that's one thing you can control. A positive attitude fosters positive performance, which produces positive results.

You can choose a grim, deadly serious, no-fun, no-frills attitude if you want. But why would you? That's no fun. It only makes work more difficult and more boring. In the phrase "deadly serious," the operative word is "deadly." Lighten up and you lighten up the load for everyone.

If you'd like a good example of a successful, playful attitude at work, look to the London-based firm called Mother. Reported to be the sexiest ad agency in the world, Mother has built an entire company on an irreverent attitude and a willingness to mock seriousness.

Poking fun at hypocrisy, pretentiousness, and other familiar foibles keeps an organization honest and more human. What school couldn't use more of that?

4. *Make their day.* If you regularly surprise and delight people and have fun at work, you build happy memories every day. That's the stuff great organizations (especially schools) are made of.

Whether it's in a fish market, an ad agency, or a public school, mixing work and fun has many positive benefits including the following:

• Fun and creativity go together. Actually, creativity is fun. It's like play with a purpose.

• Time flies when you are having fun.

• Work becomes its own reward.

• Fun is an energizer and a motivator. It's healthy and it feels good. When people have fun doing their job, they produce more, work longer and harder, and get along better with each other.

• The best employees are attracted to and stick around organizations that aren't afraid to lighten up. Fun promotes loyalty.

• Happy people make others feel good and do better. Kids do better for teachers who have fun in the classroom and make learning enjoyable. And—I've said it before—teachers do better for leaders who make work fun.

This fun thing has a lot going for it.

The benefits of the fish philosophy are available to any organization. Any leader deserving of the title makes the most of them. It starts by understanding the elements that contribute to a sense of fun at work. Here's how you tell a joyous teaching and learning environment when you see one:

• Laughter is frequent, and smiles are the norm.

• People, at all levels, laugh off their mistakes because they feel free to take risks and occasionally fall short without fear of censure.

• Everyone knows they have permission to laugh at the organization. And everyone does.

• There is a noticeable spirit of playfulness and respectful teasing. (A good sign is a high incidence of nicknames and nonthreatening practical jokes.)

Of course, these elements don't fall into place by accident. A spirit of spontaneous fun at work is often intentional from the top. The single most influential factor in determining the "enjoyment quotient" on the job—more influential than good pay and nice surroundings—is the attitude of the leader.

When bosses are fearful, defensive, paranoid, angry, self-righteous, or too full of themselves, work isn't going to be much fun that day. Or any day.

Likewise, sour superintendents or principals who take themselves too seriously naturally mold a school that is self-absorbed, pretentious, and dull. It works every time. You can't have a happy, free, and loose school with an uptight, unhappy leader.

That's the way it worked out with one superintendent I remember who was terminally tense. His demeanor was habitually serious (grim) and formal (stuffy). He didn't take coffee breaks or engage in small talk. And he begrudged the time others spent in such frivolity. He spent a lot of time looking over employees' shoulders. He demanded precise communication and exact meanings. Some staff members even took to carrying both a dictionary and a thesaurus at all times. Did I say it wasn't much fun working for him?

After a few years, he acknowledged the strained atmosphere around the office and in meetings and consciously tried to loosen things up. But he didn't know how.

He even asked subordinates to start calling him by his first name. It was too late. They couldn't do it. The culture of fear and formality was engrained.

Eventually, he moved on. A new superintendent with a lighter touch and a fondness for a good time took over, and things started humming again. Morale soared. Informality returned. So did creativity. This is not an isolated example.

As a school leader, if you enjoy your work, others will, too. Principals and superintendents don't have to be stand-up comics, great storytellers, or practical jokers. But they should model a sense of good humor and expect teachers and other employees to work hard, take pride in accomplishment—and have fun!

If you have fun, your staff will, too. If you don't—well, remember the example of the superintendent whom subordinates couldn't even call by his first name.

With the right attitude, there are many ways a school leader can foster fun in the workplace. Take your pick. You'll be glad you did. It's fun!

• Hold victory celebrations—even for small successes. Be willing to get carried away sometimes.

• Surprise staff members with special treats for no reason. Root beer floats work just fine.

• Include and involve family members in social and celebrative events at work.

• Be willing to look for the humor in all circumstances. It's always there, and it helps to make the best of a bad situation.

For example, when teachers and other staff members have to put up with the inconvenience, disruption, and dislocation of a lengthy construction project, give each one a personalized, off-the-wall, hand-decorated hard hat. It diffuses the frustration and gives everyone a trophy of the chase. At least that's the way it worked at St. Louis Park (Minnesota) High School a few years ago.

• Notice, recognize, and reward effort, not just success. That makes trying a lot more fun.

• Be willing to be the butt of jokes round school. When you make fun of yourself and allow others to do the same, you always have an appreciative audience—and you don't offend anyone.

• Promote from within whenever possible. It fosters good will and loyalty. That's fun.

• Make rallying around sick or troubled colleagues the norm.

• Let employees choose their own rewards. For some, a VIP parking space or a gift certificate might be better than a trophy.

• Promote a "club" feeling among your faculty and staff. It's fun to believe that only the best are invited to join your elite membership.

• Perform community service together as a school staff. Helping others is a special kind of fun.

- Circulate and post cartoons or jokes that relate to your school situation. (There's a reason the "Dilbert" cartoons are so popular with middle managers in the business world.)

One caution: Don't go overboard circulating e-humor over the Internet. At some point, it ceases to be funny and becomes a source of irritation. If you don't already know this from personal experience, you're lucky.

- Reinforce by word and deed that it's OK to share the humor of daily struggles, to be silly at work sometimes, to laugh loudly in the hallowed halls called school, and to find the lighter side of a demanding profession.

- Allow your school staff members to define what's fun for them. Every group is different.

Unfortunately, some educators are uncomfortable with all this talk about fun at work. They're reluctant to spend time playing on the job. They feel it is undignified and trivializes the profession. They're overreacting.

Of course, education is no laughing matter. It's not a game. It's not all play. It is probably the most important thing this nation is about. But it can be fun. In fact, it works better that way.

The point is to take the mission seriously, but not yourself. The organization that can do this is well on the way to stardom.

The best school leaders don't check laughter at the schoolhouse door. They encourage a mix of work and joy and strive to make fun a trend. Anyone can make teaching and learning more difficult. The trick is to make it easier and more enjoyable.

Remember the Pike Place Market. If there isn't something a little fishy going on at your school all the time, there should be. And that's no joke.

G Goombah and the Golden Rule

How people are treated, inspired and challenged to do their best work determines whether or not you get the most out of them.

—Bob Nelson
1001 Ways to Reward Employees

. . . being a good manager of people is not much more than using common sense and the Golden Rule—treat others as you want to be treated.

—Robert J. Nugent, CEO
Foodmaster, Inc.

The Golden Rule is of no use to you whatever unless you realize it's your move.

—Frank Crane

Want a good definition of the ideal school leader today? How about this one: *A goombah who practices the Golden Rule.* Huh? It's not as weird as it sounds.

A goombah is "an associate who acts as a patron, protector, and advisor." And the Golden Rule is, well, you know that already. Together, they make a formula for effective leadership.

There may have been a time when a principal or superintendent could pretty much get by on barking orders, making rules and "controlling" the school. Not now.

Although the temptation to control is forever strong, the only way to lead a school effectively today is by teaching, modeling, coaching, convincing, cajoling, and influencing people to win their support. That requires treating people right—like any protective goombah would—treating people the way you want to be treated. ("We're going to win on our ideas, not by using whips and chains."—Jack Welch)

But can you really run a school by the Golden Rule? You sure can. In fact, today it may be the only way to run a school (or any other organization) successfully.

It's amazing that it has taken this long to figure out that, as school leaders, how you act toward the school staff is the chief determiner of how they will react to you. You get what you give.

If there really is a secret to success for school administrators, you won't find it in your favorite graduate program. You'll find it in your family Bible. It's the Golden Rule. And it will work for you in your school.

Don't scoff. This isn't something you just have to accept on faith. Repeated studies have shown that behavior is reciprocal. If you treat your staff with honesty, respect, and civility, they will respond in kind. People give back what they get. What goes around comes around. That's the magic of the Golden Rule.

In researching his book *1001 Ways to Reward Employees*, Bob Nelson found that winning companies obtained results "precisely because of how they treated people." In those organizations where employees are treated fairly and respectfully, employees like coming to work, their morale is high, they do their best without being told, and everyone feels their contribution makes a difference. It can work exactly the same way in your school.

As a principal or superintendent, how you treat your people is more important than what you know. Productivity in any organization is largely the result of the relationship between the leader and the followers. In tough times, this relationship is even more important.

People respond to leaders not for who the leaders are, but for how their leaders make them feel. Employees—including teachers and other staff members—develop loyalty to a person—an individual (principal or superintendent)—not to an amorphous organization (the school). Without a positive relationship between leaders and followers, nothing positive happens and any new ideas or initiatives are met with suspicion.

The only way school leaders can get the commitment and support they want and need is to give them away. Treat your people right, and they will propel you to success. It can't happen any other way today.

Meeting the needs of the school requires meeting the needs of all those working in the school. But first, you have to understand what it is that teachers and other staff members really need. That's why it pays to personally get to know as many people as possible, as well as possible—not just teachers, but everyone from the top to the bottom of the organization.

As principal or superintendent, the most important currency you have is your relationship with all those who work in the school. The quality of that relationship defines the quality of everything the school does.

Relationship building requires some personal contact. It is difficult for teachers or other personnel to relate to a voice over the intercom, an impersonal memo, or a stream of e-mail messages. They need to get to know their leader directly, personally, face-to-face—as an individual—before a truly effective relationship can be forged.

In a small school, this is easy. But even in a large school, there are ways to make personal and direct contact with all of your teachers, clerks, custodians, cooks, and other staff members. Hiding out in your office isn't one of them.

The best school leaders make contact with everyone on their staff on a regular basis. Sometimes it takes significant extra effort. Here are a few measures that have helped some of your colleagues:

• Keep a chart logging weekly or monthly contact with all staff members. Where gaps occur, purposely seek out those with whom you don't regularly interact. (It worked for one of my mentors, Dr. Stan Wignes, at Central Junior High in suburban Minneapolis.)

• Personally hand-deliver paychecks to your staff. That guarantees at least one positive contact with every person twice each month.

• Park in a different space and enter or leave through a different entrance once in awhile. It's a good way to get exposed to some staffers you ordinarily wouldn't see.

• Make Fridays "How Are You Doin'? Day" Invite employees, who are usually out of sight and out of mind, to lunch—just to share feelings, opinions, impressions, frustrations, perceptions, and ideas.

If you get to know everyone on your staff—know their first names and something about their lives—you will have a better school. Guaranteed.

I became a believer after observing a deputy superintendent in Topeka, Kansas, who, when visiting any school in the district, could call each employee by name and refer to something specific about his or her work, family, or life outside of school.

That act alone was a powerful motivating force felt throughout the system. It's hard not to connect and commit to an organization in which the top brass calls you by name.

Of course, getting to know your staff members isn't the same thing as meeting their needs or treating them as you want to be treated. You still actually have to do something.

It's like a dog chasing a car. What would the dog do if it actually caught one? What do you do once you're in touch with what's going on with your employees? How do you really run a school according to the Golden Rule?

There are lots of ways to be a good goombah, but the following eight steps are essential to building a Golden Rule relationship with your entire school staff. They're fail-safe and foolproof. They will work if you care and dare enough to try them.

1. *Meet basic psychological and emotional needs.* There are many lists of basic human needs. Here is my favorite: activity, ownership, power, affiliation, competence, achievement, recognition, meaning, and fun.

If you create an environment that satisfies these needs, you will not only have happy campers, you will have the most exciting, innovative, and productive campsite around. I don't know why they don't teach this in graduate school.

2. *Overinvest in people.* Be lavish with trust, praise, freedom, support, and encouragement. But also customize your emotional compensation to meet each employee's individual situation.

3. *Make every staff member feel special.* Appreciate everyone's contribution. Show it. People will do wonders if they are appreciated and even more if they are thanked. (Some of the most effective leaders I've known have told me that they say "thank you" at least 20 times a day.)

4. *Treat everyone with dignity and respect.* Listen. Be accessible. Don't pull rank. Show staff members that they are needed. Never keep them in the dark. Don't treat teachers like children. (They hate it.) Don't waste their time. Respect their life away from the school.

5. *Trust people.* ("Trust is the emotional glue that binds followers and leaders together."—Warren Bemis) When employees are trusted, they feel that

- Administration is interested in me as an individual.
- My work contributes.
- I am treated fairly.
- My values are shared by others.

Do your staff members feel that way? If not, why not? When principals, superintendents, teachers, and other staff members trust each other, no one wants to work anywhere else. You can't buy that kind of loyalty.

6. *Give credit.* Leaders have to give credit away to get any in return. You don't claim credit. It claims you. Effective leaders admit mistakes, accept blame, and give away 100 percent of the credit for successes.

7. *Empower people.* (It's a cliché. But it's a truthful one.) Give employees a voice. Invite them to take responsibility. Give them permission to make the organization better.

Some may not take the bait. I remember an elementary principal who once told me, "I don't want any more empowerment. Just tell me what to do." That's OK, but just having the opportunity matters.

Empowerment means not requiring all teachers to teach alike. (That's coercion, not empowerment.) It also means knowing when not to meddle or interfere. As business guru Ken Blanchard admonishes, "Don't just do something, stand there." Empowerment works because it allows people to show what they can do.

8. *Give employees an "ownership attitude."* When staff members think, act, and worry like an owner, they take a greater personal interest in outcomes and results and think more about how what they do affects the overall school. It's an attitude that can help make you a winner. It's an attitude worth sharing with your colleagues and coworkers at all levels.

Applying these concepts can make you a better leader and transform your school into a more distinctive, unusual, and special place to work and learn. They are indeed that powerful.

If you need more specifics, following are some concrete examples of ways to flesh out these principles and bring the Golden Rule to life within your learning organization:

• Apply the lesson contained in Connie Podesta's compelling book, *Self-Esteem and the 6-Second Secret.* Most administrators and other supervisors spend a lot more time complaining, than complimenting (e.g., typically 6 seconds of praise for every 60 seconds of criticism or complaint). Try reversing that ratio. It will multiply your impact.

• Give responsible recognition. People tend to live up to the recognition they receive. School personnel are no exception. But all awards or rewards should be timely, specific, and appropriate to the achievement. They should also be presented in person and in public whenever possible. Avoid any recognition that is too slick, too rehearsed, or too embarrassing.

And be sure to recognize contributions from all categories of employees, not just teachers (e.g., if you give teachers their own personalized business cards, do the same for clerks, custodians, and others).

• Find ways to introduce more flexibility into your staff's working environment. According to a recent survey by Robert Half International, 66 percent of all workers would take a pay cut in exchange for more flexibility. That percentage could be even higher among teachers who are classroom-bound most of the time. Anything you can do to get teachers out of their regular routine periodically and to experiment with flexible scheduling for classified personnel will be appreciated.

Allowing and encouraging flexibility is another area in which school leaders can take a tip from business leaders such as Karen Oman, president of Certes Financial Pros. Oman received *Working Woman* magazine's "Best Employer" award in 2000 for her flexible scheduling of employees. At Certes, employees can take up to half a year off to tend to personal business without losing benefits.

You may not be able to go that far in your school, but you can allow a lot more flexibility than most schools enjoy today. Any added flexibility pays off in increased effort, commitment, and loyalty.

As Oman, who writes business poetry as a hobby, explains,

> *Saying "no" is easy;*
> *It keeps the status quo's,*
> *But people leave to meet their needs*
> *As everyone knows . . .*
> *If you choose to give an inch*
> *They won't want a mile . . .*
> *Instead, you'll grow grand loyalty.*
> *They'll thrive and do their best . . .*
> *For when you give their needs respect*
> *You've passed their "leader" test!*

(After reading this, you understand why I wasn't surprised to learn that Oman frequently passes out golden rulers, like calling cards, with the inscription, "Treat others as you would want to be treated . . . Works in business too.")

• Send handwritten notes. They stand out and make a lasting impression. Use them to praise, congratulate, say thank-you, express sympathy, or just pass on an FYI. But don't use them to vent anger. A nasty note will come back to bite you every time.

While you're at it, why not improve your handwriting? Most school clerical personnel have trouble reading their boss's writing. Illegible or sloppy writing is inconsiderate, wastes time and money, and causes errors and embarrassment. You can do better.

• Use technology respectfully. Many of today's technological wonders can actually work against you. If misused, overused, or abused, technology makes it too easy for administrators to micromanage, butt in, or "e-noy" others.

By any conservative estimate, half of all e-mail sent in schools has no meaningful, educational, or otherwise worthwhile purpose. Yet most people feel obligated to respond.

You hate to be inundated with Internet clutter. Other people feel the same way, so don't contribute to the glut. Send messages only for a good reason. Check your e-words carefully. And limit the numbers of FYIs you forward.

The same respectful use should apply to voicemail messages. Keep them short. Even an extra 10 seconds can be an irritant.

• Be creative with titles. Use them to identify and highlight genuine contributions. For example, with the realization that a good receptionist is worth a million dollars to any organization, an ingenious city administrator switched the title to "Director of First Impressions." Can you come up with similar titles that accurately reflect the real contributions your non-teaching staff members make to the school's success? Try it. You (and your staff) will be glad you did.

Of course, the list of possible applications of the Golden Rule could go on and on, but you get the point. You know how you want to be treated by superiors. Take that information and pass it down—make it the way you relate to all of your employees. There is no recorded instance in which enforcing the Golden Rule has backfired or made things worse.

Suggesting that you treat people as you want to be treated isn't just wishful thinking, idealistic sermonizing, or warm-fuzzy psychobabble. It's bread-and-butter survival advice. If you're not following it, you're missing a fundamental precept of good leadership.

Reciprocal behavior is compelling. Psychologists have known for a long time that we all have an urge to return treatment in kind. Studies even show that if shouted at, most people can't control the impulse to shout back. Our behavior just naturally echoes the way others behave toward us. That's why the Golden Rule will work in your school—not maybe will work, but *will* work.

So if you are not happy with what you're getting from your school staff, whose fault is it? Things can get better. But it won't happen by itself. It's your move, goombah!

History
and Heroes

. . . organizations don't run on rules, but on stories.

—Dale Dauten
syndicated business columnist

Without heroes, we're all plain people and don't know how far we can go.

—Bernard Malamud
writer

Some leaders try to divorce themselves from the past. They want to ignore history and fiercely forge ahead into the future. They're missing a good bet!

The most successful organizations—the ones that achieve eminence in their field and stay there—build on their legends; perpetuate their winning culture through traditions, rituals, and stories (tales of past heroes and maybe a few scapegoats and villains as well); and use their history to illuminate where they've been and where they want to go. ("We can chart our future clearly and wisely only when we know the path which has led to the present."—Adlai Stevenson)

History and heroes can be powerful tools for moving an organization forward. It's true of nations. It's true of businesses. And it's especially true of schools.

The effective leader understands and uses the power of the past. The flash in the pan never quite figures it out.

This point was forcibly driven home for me early in my career when I was part of an administrative team assigned to open a second high school in Topeka, Kansas (Topeka West High School). The facilities, the furnishings and the equipment were all brand new. The students were drawn from the city's only existing high school, which had served the community well for almost 100 years.

In my naiveté, I assumed the students would be excited to be part of something so new—to be trailblazers with the opportunity to select new school colors, pick out a mascot, name the school paper and yearbook, and create new ways of doing things. I was wrong.

The kids—especially the seniors—hated it. They felt betrayed, abandoned, and disenfranchised. They resented having no traditions to guide them and no history to live up to. They were envious of the students who remained in the old school with its established structure and patterns. Instead of being excited about new opportunities, they anguished over the loss of precedents.

Of course, things got better over time as the students and staff built a history together. But the lesson of the importance of roots and rituals has stuck with me. Now it's yours for the taking.

Successful organizations—including your school—must continuously outdo themselves. History can help. A rich history gives everyone something to equal and surpass.

History connects students and staff to the school. It humanizes and personalizes the institution and makes it a more lively and interesting place to work and learn. Without a history, there is no sense of the past or the future. (Remember Topeka West High School.)

Stories of heroes help put a face on the school's vision. They create an environment in which everyone can be proud of what they do, what others do, and what the organization stands for.

History builds morale and motivates people at all levels. Knowing about the organization's heritage satisfies the basic human need for affiliation and for being involved in something important. It makes everyone on the payroll feel as if they are part of an exclusive club. For some, that is worth more than a salary increase.

Best of all, historical perspective allows the organization to "fail forward" by learning from past mistakes. What's happened in the past can help those in the present understand what to do and what not to do in the future.

Healthy plants have strong roots. So do healthy organizations. That includes schools. All human institutions constantly evolve and change over time. But the ones that survive remain true to their roots and build on their history. If that's not happening in your school, it should be.

Successful businesses have always traded on their past by using the history of the organization to give credibility to the present. It's no accident that Ford Motor Company makes a big deal out of the legacy of Henry Ford's vision and innovative contributions. Likewise, it is strictly intentional when the Wells Fargo Bank capitalizes on its colorful history (remember the streaking stage coach) to convey an image of vitality and excitement for their operations today.

The examples are everywhere. If you are skeptical, just check the number of television commercials that refer to heroic figures or signature events out of the advertiser's history. (While you're at it, notice how many "reunion shows" television networks stage to commemorate hit shows from the past.)

Good businesses always make the most of their history. They use the past to build a better future. Should schools do the same? You bet.

Every school—even a relatively new one—has its own set of heroes and inspiring historical moments that can be put to good use. You don't have to be around for a hundred years to have a powerful past. Yesterday is history enough for all those who didn't live it.

The trick is to know how to use the school's past to the greatest advantage in the present. Three tips from veteran administrators can help:

1. Tell the school's story as often as you can in as many ways as you can (e.g., develop a written history, produce a video of historical highlights, and have students create a mural depicting important events in the school's past).

It also helps if you are a good storyteller. Storytelling is a powerful tool for passing on values, saying more with less, creating a common understanding of what's important, and forging a shared purpose.

2. Select your heroes carefully. The kind of people you honor says a lot about the kind of organization you were, are, and will become.

3. Differentiate between valuable history and excess baggage. Not all people and events are worth remembering.

There are lots of ways to capitalize on history and make history at the same time. You know administrators who do it all the time. You should, too.

Here are some simple starter suggestions for keeping your school's history alive and well, while building your own legacy to pass on to the future:

• Create a School Hall of Fame (or, at least, a Wall of Fame) highlighting achievements of outstanding alumni (including former staff members).

• Play up homecoming celebrations and class reunions. Some schools have success scheduling targeted reunions (e.g., everyone who ever played or coached football for the school).

• Help establish a Teacher Hall of Fame in your state and nominate some of your outstanding former teachers for induction. (The Kansas Teacher Hall of Fame in Emporia, Kansas, can serve as a model. Contact Emporia State University for more information.)

• Hold a Trivial Pursuit Contest based on historical trivia about your school.

• Make a fuss over digging up time capsules buried by former students or classes. And bury some new ones of your own.

• Keep trophy shelves up-to-date and showcased in a prominent place in the school.

• Invite celebrity alumni to come back to address student and staff groups.

• Partner with your local historical society to develop a school museum.

• Initiate and maintain an active alumni association and create a School Foundation so that successful alumni can designate endowments to benefit the school in the future.

• Name facilities after prominent former students, teachers, or administrators.

• Establish a Peace Garden at your school in memory of former students and staff members.

• Create new heroes. Publicize everyone's successes. Let employees recognize each other and choose their own form of reward. Use unusual recognition events to create a story that employees and students can share with others.

• Let students nominate new heroes (outstanding employees) for recognition—not just teachers, but anyone who serves the school. (In St. Louis Park, Minnesota, students at the Susan Lindgren Intermediate Center selected a custodian as the recipient of the school's initial Children First Award.)

It's not difficult to keep the school's history fresh. But it does take conscious effort. It's worth it. After all, your history is your reputation. It is important.

Every school starts out with an aura of energy of excitement. It's the school leader's job to preserve that promise and pass it on. In times of instability, rapid change, fragmentation, and disconnection, a sense of history may be more important than ever.

Of course, there are always a few principals and superintendents who choose to downplay the past because they want to be the primary heroes who are recognized and remembered in the school. They miss the point of Will Rogers' observation: "Being a hero is about the shortest-lived profession on earth." Those who set out to make themselves a hero seldom become one.

As leader, you can choose to ignore the school's history and past heroes. You can also tie one hand behind your back. But why would you want to?

The best way to be your best is to use every tool at your disposal, including legacies from the past. You will be a better leader if you preserve the school's past. Use it. Celebrate it. And build on it—but don't live in it!

Inform, Instruct, and Inspire

I make beanstalks. I'm a builder.

—Edna St. Vincent Millay
poet

Quality is never accidental.

—John Ruskin
writer and art critic

Good management consists in showing average people how to do the work of superior people.

—John D. Rockefeller
oil magnate

Most of us might agree that one of the best three-word job descriptions for a teacher is simply, "Inform, Instruct, and Inspire." But would you agree that it applies equally well to principals and superintendents?

You should. Effective school leaders inform, instruct, and inspire, too. In fact, if you can master these three I-functions, you can pretty much run any school or district in the country.

Principals and superintendents have a great deal in common with the staff members they supervise. They all teach. The main difference is that administrators are always teaching a multitude of subjects simultaneously, and their student body is everybody within the school community. To succeed, school leaders must be teachers of teachers—and of parents and the entire community—as well as of students.

It's nothing new. Good leaders have always been good teachers. Jesus did a lot of informing, instructing, and inspiring. So did Gandhi. So have all successful leaders in all fields. And so do you if you're doing the job right.

The three I-functions are time-honored building blocks of leadership. But each of these traditional functions now has some added new twists.

In today's Information Age, the function of informing has taken on a whole new meaning. Peter Drucker (recipient of the Presidential Medal of Freedom who was described by President George W. Bush as "the foremost pioneer of management theory") started it all by first coining the term "knowledge workers" in 1969. It stuck.

The implication is that employees in all organizations need to be better informed and more knowledgeable than ever before. Of course, it's up to leaders to see that it happens.

Workers in all fields need to know a lot more than just how to do their jobs. They also need (in fact, many demand) to be informed about all facets of the organization, including detailed financial data. If you think this doesn't apply to teachers and other school staff members, you're living in the wrong millennium.

Information is power. Naturally, everyone wants it. The smartest leaders in schools, in businesses, and elsewhere are increasingly willing to spread knowledge around, because *information shared is power multiplied.* (Reread that last sentence one more time—slowly. If there were a chapter test, this would be on it.)

The days when manipulative managers could hoard information and ration it out according to whim are long gone. (Believe it or not, some school administrators operated this way in the past. A few still do.)

Information isn't a perk reserved for management. It belongs to everyone in the organization. And the sooner it is disseminated, the better.

Despite the qualms of some insecure principals and superintendents, there are several compelling reasons for keeping everyone in the organization fully informed about the organization. Here are the top seven:

1. *Sharing information is the key to empowerment.* No one can make sound decisions without it. Absent complete knowledge, teachers and other employees cannot be held responsible or accountable.

2. *Informed personnel work harder and are more productive.* ("It's a funny thing about human nature. We generally do better work if we know what the hell we're doing and why the hell we're doing it."—James Carville)

3. *Keeping everyone in the loop builds morale.* Conversely, one surefire way to turn top performers into grousing malcontents is to shut them

out. Letting people in on what's happening is critical to attracting and retaining talent.

4. *Informed employees care more.* Having full access to information encourages everyone on board to feel, think, and act like an owner.

5. *Information sharing builds trust, establishes credibility, and breaks down bureaucratic mind-sets.*

6. *Full disclosure creates unity.* It demonstrates courage, commitment, and good faith on the part of administration. When employees at all levels feel that "we're in this together," loyalty and teamwork naturally follow.

7. *When subordinates are treated as "associates" (rather than lackeys) and are allowed to see how the organization really works, they can help make it work even better.*

That's why some principals regularly invite employees—not just teachers, but all employees—to shadow them for a day (Principal-for-a-Day Program) to see more clearly what really makes the entire school tick.

Obviously, it takes a certain amount of courage to disclose everything. But it takes even more to try to explain to teacher leaders and union officials why you aren't doing it. The bottom line is that when you give people all the information they want and need, good things happen. When you don't, nothing happens.

Of course, the demand for disclosure is not limited to teachers and other staff members. Parents and community members are also increasingly pressing to find out more about what's going on in the schools.

New demands for information call for bold, new initiatives. The following examples may trigger your thinking about fresh possibilities within your own school situation:

• Even before the scourge of corporate scandals in 2002 (e.g., Enron, Worldcom, etc.), many schools and businesses had introduced Open Book Management. Opening up financial records to all employees and sharing all budgetary information is the first step in developing an "ownership culture" in which all stakeholders feel positively connected to the organization.

After all, the budget is supposed to be a tool, not a secret. When employees have the same access to financial data that management has, trust happens.

I first learned this lesson during a contentious series of contract negotiations. As long as both sides of the table tried to hide information from each other, tempers sizzled and impasse ensued. When we decided to share and freely exchange information and give the unions access to all the financial data the district was using, settlement became a possibility.

Of course, information sharing won't convert collective bargaining into a nonadversarial process. But it will speed it up. More important, it builds a bond of mutual trust and respect that transcends normal labor disputes.

• Another new wrinkle is to start informing staff members even before they are hired. Traditionally, most principals and superintendents have gone out of their way to put their best foot forward with potential new hires (the "First-Date Syndrome") by hiding bad news and downplaying problem areas.

More and more of your peers are now finding that a better way is to tell future teachers and other employees the whole truth upfront—warts and all—the good, the bad, and the ugly. It's a way to establish credibility from Day 1.

If prospective employees want utopia, they may have to die and go to heaven. If they want a real job, they have to accept a few challenges. That's why we call it work.

• Sometimes, the best way for school leaders to perform the informing function is to let someone else do it. One effective approach is to let students inform the broader community about problems and needs instead of doing it yourself.

For example, when students in suburban Minneapolis decided that adults in the community needed to hear directly from them about what kinds of support kids need today, they did something about it.

In hope of initiating an intergenerational dialogue, the students compiled *An Adult's Guide to Kids* and distributed it to every household throughout the community. That's informing the public! No principal or superintendent could do it better.

Likewise, some communities have found yet another vehicle for engaging students to inform the public—a Mayor's Youth Summit. Typically, a Youth Summit provides an opportunity for kids to talk and for adults to listen—the reverse of most public forums. Topics usually include relevant youth issues such as safe streets, rites of passage, or "nothing to do."

At the summit, the youth's job is to open up and candidly discuss what's going on in the school and the community from the kids' perspective, what's working, what's not, and what needs fixing. The adults' role is strictly to listen to what the young people are saying and feeling, without interruption, intervention, interrogation, or editorializing.

School leaders could convey the same things that the kids present. But when it comes from kids, adults listen—and hear. That's what informing the public is all about.

With so many people clamoring for more and more data and details, the informing function of leadership could easily become a full-time occupation. But there's more—much more. School leaders also have a lot of instructing to do.

According to most dictionaries, instruction involves both teaching (imparting knowledge) and giving authoritative directions (orders and instructions). Every school leader you and I know has plenty of both to do.

For starters, the teachers who come to you may already know a lot. But there's still a great deal they don't know about your organization. It's your job to teach them about the dreams, vision, mission, goals, history, culture, promises, and possibilities of your particular school. Sometimes you have to teach them the tools and tricks of the trade. Other times, you may have to help them unlearn bad habits or faulty lessons learned elsewhere.

Likewise, as principal or superintendent, it's your responsibility to teach each new generation of parents about school rules and roles and to educate the community about the real purpose of the school and what it can become.

There is always more to teach. And it's always important, because "if people don't get it right, they can't do it right."

For most school leaders today, the problem isn't what instruction to give, but how to give it. The way instruction is presented is as important as the content. It spells the difference between making meaningful connections and missing the mark. Unfortunately, teachers are not always the best pupils and don't always follow instructions so well.

Instructing adults (especially adults who are teachers themselves) can be tricky business. The secret is simply to treat adults as adults. Teach without preaching and challenge them to grow without resorting to harsh judgments, demeaning criticism, or embarrassing "mind games."

What usually works best is to focus on outcomes rather than minute details or prescriptive procedures. Give options, not formulas. ("Never tell people how to do things. Tell them what to do and they will surprise you with their ingenuity."—Gen. George S. Patton)

Certain critical situations may also require scheduling individual face time with each stakeholder to ensure that they "get it."

It never hurts to bring in reinforcements. Some principals have had success recruiting retired teachers (elders of the tribe) to pass on the wisdom of their experience. Sometimes teachers tune out what administrators have to say but will listen to other teachers. Done correctly, informing and instructing take a lot of every principal's and superintendent's time. So much so, that some administrators call that the whole job and stop right there. Unfortunately, they're stopping one step short of leadership. They leave out the most important of the three I-functions—Inspiring!

Any manager or bureaucrat can pass on information or dish out directives. But it takes a genuine leader to inspire an organization to change from what it is to what it ought to be.

If all you ever achieve as the leader of your school is to inspire people to be and do their best and to raise the organization to a higher level, that's enough for one lifetime. There is no greater gift any leader can give than an ideal that excites people's emotions and energizes them to take action to improve. Leaders never stop raising the bar. We've all heard that good scouts always leave the campsite better than they found it. Good leaders do the same.

Too many organizations—including most schools—underdefine themselves. When the standard is set too low, it's the leader's fault.

When the renowned Jack Welch was in charge of General Electric, one of his favorite mantras was "Being Number 1 or Number 2 isn't an objective, it's a requirement." That wouldn't be a bad gospel to preach to your school.

If you have the makings of a true leader, you are not interested in running a mediocre school. Let it show. Steadfastly demonstrating that you won't settle for second best is how you move an organization from aspiration to inspiration.

You don't have to be a larger-than-life human dynamo, a fiery orator, or a charismatic phenomenon to inspire others to exceed the ordinary. But you do have to set high standards and stick to them.

Don't measure your school's success against the average. Benchmark against the best and then benchmark against yourself. Why settle for anything less than world-class performance?

Everyone knows who the gold standard companies are in the business world (e.g., Disney, Southwest Airlines, etc.). And every principal and superintendent you know can name the gold standard schools in your area. If yours isn't one of them, why not? It could be.

Inspiring peak performance also means defining the right outcomes, helping people find out how they fit in, and making the challenge real by showing you mean it every day.

Believe it or not, for most educators, money is not the prime mover and motivator in their career. The best teachers, administrators, and other school staff members everywhere are looking for something deeper— some greater purpose or meaning. They want an idea or an ideal worth working for. Give it to them. That's all inspiration amounts to.

You can't inform people into being passionate, and you can't teach passion. But you can inspire people to be passionate about their work. When you do, magic happens. Any of you who have ever worked with an inspirational leader know what I'm talking about.

Like many of you, I've experienced firsthand the power of a passionate leader. While under his tutelage, my colleagues and I walked a little taller and worked a little harder. We made gains we wouldn't have believed possible before. We knew when we crossed over from good to great. Others noticed, too.

I distinctly remember when a department head from a prestigious neighboring school system once asked me, "When did your district decide to be Number 1?" I don't know exactly what I replied then, but I know the right answer: It was at the very moment our leader convinced us that we could be. That's what inspiration can do for an organization.

There you have it: The three I-functions—Leadership 101 in a nutshell. Ultimately, all the world's complicated theories and explanations of leadership boil down to these three simple words: "Inform, Instruct, and Inspire." Now that you know it, somebody should tell the education professors in graduate school.

J Jacks or Better

Timing is everything. It is as important to know when as to know how.

—Arnold Glasow

Better three hours too soon, than one minute late.

—William Shakespeare
playwright

In poker, regular players don't play their cards unless or until they have some potential for a winning hand—at least, a pair of jacks or better. Effective leaders do the same thing.

It's not just in a card game that you need to know "when to hold 'em, when to fold 'em and when to walk away." It's in everyday living as well. Who would have thought that poker would turn out to be a metaphor for living and leading?

Sooner or later (sooner is better), every successful leader learns that timing is everything. It's one of the fundamental and universal laws of leadership. In case you blinked and missed it, it bears repeating—*TIMING IS EVERYTHING.*

We've all seen good ideas fail, sound programs fail, even promising leaders fail, because of bad timing. When the timing is right, you can accomplish wonders. When the timing is wrong, forget it.

As a principal or supervisor, if you move too soon or too quickly, people aren't ready. If you wait too long or move too slowly, you may miss the window of opportunity. There's a right and wrong time for everything.

That's why good leaders have to develop a sense of timing. It requires exercising patience, being realistic, paying attention, reading the signs, gauging reactions, and trusting your gut. It's not a sixth sense. It's mostly common sense.

It also pays to be a trend spotter—identify what's coming, how fast and how soon. (Take a tip from software maven and billionaire, Bill Gates: "People often overestimate what will happen in the next two years and underestimate what will happen in ten.") Don't worry. Experience will boost your forecasting skills.

Once you understand the impact that timing has on everything, everything gets easier, and you become a more effective school leader.

Of course, knowing or sensing when the time is right to act is useless unless you are prepared to capitalize on the opportunity. (As it turns out, readiness isn't just for reading. It's essential for leading as well.) And it should be no surprise that opportunities usually come to those most ready to seize the moment.

Fortunately, there are measures that can help position you and your school to take advantage of propitious timing. If you don't implement them, someone else will. It could be the school next door.

When you really want to learn how to set your school up to respond better to opportunities (or threats), look to your business counterparts. Business leaders invented timing. They had to.

In today's fierce economic competition, good timing is all that separates winners from losers. Businesses have to be ready to act promptly and appropriately when the time is right. In the modern global economy, there are only two kinds of businesses: the quick and the dead.

That's why a lot of downsizing has occurred. That's why many companies have flattened out their organizational chart. That's why many businesses are breaking down barriers between departments and divisions. That's the reason Jack Welch, retired CEO, brags about General Electric's "boundaryless" organization.

Obviously, you should never be too proud to borrow good ideas about timing (or anything else) from successful businesses. The best school leaders do it all the time.

Here's what many leading businesses (and leading schools) do to make themselves more prepared to act or react in a timely manner to any development:

• *Hoard ideas.* Good ideas can come from anywhere, at any time. So, read voraciously. Listen. Observe. Keep your antennae out. Save ideas originally discarded in brainstorming. Their time may come yet.

You would be surprised by how many school leaders keep an idea file or notebook. What do they know that you don't?

Good ideas always find their time if someone is ready to run with them when the time is right. Be ready.

- *Become a bureaucracy buster.* Remove excess layers of decision making. Reduce the number of intermediaries (associate superintendents, assistant principals, directors, coordinators, department heads) wherever possible. Good ideas shouldn't have to go to too many places to get approval.

Many cutting-edge businesses are trying to make their organization look less like a ladder and more like a lattice. How about trying that in your school?

- *Empower people at all levels.* (I know it's an overworked, corny cliché. But it works.) Teach others how to be less dependent on you. Give teachers and other staff members the freedom and authority to act, make choices, and reach decisions within their defined area of responsibility. Then, make them accountable for their actions.

Good leaders point employees in the right direction and get out of their way. Poor leaders only get in the way.

Your school's timing will never be what it should be as long as people in the organization always have to wait for your permission to move ahead.

- *Encourage cross-training.* Arrange for staff members to learn each other's jobs. It will make the organization more flexible, responsive, and adaptive. That's a good thing.

- *Create cross-functional, self-directed teams.* More and more businesses are relying on interdisciplinary groups of employees to plan, implement, manage, and make decisions about selected projects from start to finish. Usually, these teams have the freedom to pick their own leader and make their own rules. It adds another dimension to "empowerment" by moving decision making closer to where the action is needed and speeding up response time.

This is too good an idea to waste on businesses. It works in schools, too. Yours can be next.

Teams can't replace leadership. But they can be an extension—an extra arm—of leadership. Couldn't you use another arm in your job?

- *Keep everyone in the loop.* If everyone is fully informed, you don't have to waste time getting people up to speed when the right time to act presents itself. This is so obvious, it's almost embarrassing to mention. But there are still some principals and superintendents who think it's their job to hoard information and ration it out according to their whim. This not only slows down their timing; it stops it dead in its tracks.

• *Develop a culture of responsibility.* In an ideal school, all staff members understand that if they see a problem, it is their responsibility to try to fix it or get someone who can. The old excuses—It's not my job, They're not my students, This is not my assigned area—won't float.

When everyone is responsible for the whole organization, no one waits for someone else to tackle problems. They do it themselves. On the spot. Right now. That's good timing.

• *Eliminate confusion, overcome bottlenecks, and streamline tasks.* Confusion is a blocker. When people have to waste time figuring out what to do, good timing goes out the window. Make things clear and keep things simple. It works every time.

• *Don't always have to have a meeting.* Too many businesses (and too many schools) have too many meetings. If you don't think it's true in your situation, check your calendar. The old saying, "Winners do, losers meet," is a lesson in good timing.

Don't get married to your conference room. If you always have to wait for a meeting before anything can happen, not much will happen. The time-honored business principle, "A meeting moves at the speed of the slowest mind in the room," applies to schools, too.

Enough said. The fewer the meetings, the quicker your response time.

Good timing doesn't just happen. It takes skill. You can get better at this. The steps provided here and other similar strategies will increase your school's capacity to respond, adjust, adapt, shift gears, reverse course, or switch directions easily, smoothly, and quickly. It also helps if you keep in mind the following Ten Rules for Good Timing:

1. *There is no perfect time.* Don't wait until everything is perfect before you act. If you do, you will be permanently stuck in the status quo. Nature abhors perfection. It never happens.

Wait for the most favorable odds you're likely to get, and then go for it. Take what you can get. ("Half a loaf is still bread."—Peter Drucker, management guru.)

2. *Quicker is better.* When the time is right to make your move, it pays to move quickly. ("There is a correlation between speed and excellence."—James Carville)

If you're not familiar with the term "alacrity," it's a word and a concept you need to know about. It means promptness in response—moving from decision to action quickly. If you doubt that this is a critical trait for successful organizations, check out *It's Not the Big That Eat the Small. It's the Fast That Eat the Slow* by Jason Jennings and Laurence Houghton (HarperCollins).

Making right choices fast and acting on them quickly are among the toughest parts of any school leader's job. Of course, there's a difference between acting quickly and acting hastily. If you don't know what that difference is, it's time to go back to Good Timing School.

The trick is to be fast, informed, and focused—all at once. Notice that "fast" comes first. ("The quicker you let go of old cheese, the sooner you enjoy new cheese."—Spencer Johnson, MD)

3. *It's also OK to wait (if you wait for the right reasons).* Never act for action's sake. If necessary, hold off and take your time to learn, weigh options, build relationships, make allies, or develop strategies.

Sometimes, the time is right to procrastinate. A purposeful pause in the action or a little intentional drifting can be a good thing. ("Not all who wander are lost."—J. R. R. Tolkien)

4. *When it's over, it's over.* Know when to bury a dead horse. If an idea's time has not yet come or has come and gone, don't throw more money at it or waste more time on it. Move on.

Of course, some principals and superintendents are too stubborn to give up on any of their ideas or projects. They will do almost anything rather than admit that their horse has expired. As one anonymous Internet writer explains (with tongue in cheek), "When you discover that you are riding a dead horse, the best strategy is to dismount." But in modern business (or education or government), other strategies are being tried with dead horses including the following:

- Buying a new whip.
- Appointing a committee to study dead horses.
- Lowering standards to include dead horses.
- Providing additional funding to improve the dead horse's performance.

And as a final strategy . . .

- *Promoting the dead horse to a management position.*

There is no better time to abandon what's not working than this very minute.

5. *Instincts are worth following.* Your gut can tell you when the time is right. ("Trust your hunches. They're usually based on facts filed away just below the conscious level."—Joyce Brothers, psychologist)

6. *You can never get everybody on board at once.* Don't wait until everyone is with your program before you move ahead. Eternity is a long time

to wait around. ("Schools can and must move forward without everyone on the train—but there will be more people on the train if it is clear where it is going."—Anonymous)

7. *Proaction is better than reaction.* The time is always right to get the jump on opportunities or to prevent problems. It beats knee-jerk management every time.

8. *Crawl, walk, run.* In most circumstances, good timing means following this natural progression, allowing enough time for each phase.

9. *Sometimes you can create your own timing.* Good timing isn't always a matter of passively waiting for the stars to come into proper alignment. Sometimes you have to nudge conditions a little.

Some leaders have been known to create a little chaos in times of excessive calm. Some have even gone so far as to manufacture an emergency to jar jaded professionals into action.

It's more common for a leader to try to speed up glacial movement by bypassing intermediaries, established channels or traditional hierarchies to intervene directly. You're allowed to do that when you are the boss— whatever you can do to create the right time to act is OK.

10. *Remain true to your mission.* How do you know when to act? When it moves you closer to your dream. When it helps kids. The vision of the school should be the first checkpoint before taking any action.

Obviously, timing is tricky business. But it's your business. All successful school leaders have a sense of timing. Bogus leaders don't have a clue.

Leadership isn't a card game. But, like poker, winning depends a lot more on timing than on luck. (Remember jacks or better to open.)

Don't lose your edge by default. Pay attention to timing. You'll always be glad you did.

You can't be a genius all the time. But you can be sometimes. The trick is to know when.

Did I mention that timing is everything?

 **"Kick Butt and Hug"**

I must be cruel to be kind.

—William Shakespeare
playwright

Sometimes you have to kick ass to get people to do the right thing.

—*The District*
television series

J ack Welch, arguably the nation's most famous retired CEO (General Electric), preaches that leaders have to "kick butt and hug." Not just business leaders, but all leaders—even school leaders.

Of course as educators, we are "professionals." We prefer to say that we motivate and nurture or that we practice progressive discipline and positive reinforcement. It's the same thing.

Basically, it's the old "carrot and stick" approach all over again. And it works in schools just as well as in factories, shops, and offices. But it's a little trickier in schools.

What Welch means is that effective leaders, in all fields, have to be a cattle prod, a mother confessor, and a cheerleader. Sometimes, they need to be hard-nosed and aggressive, at other times warm and generous. And while they are at it, they have to be tough-minded and straightforward all the time.

I hate to admit it, but business leaders often do a better job of this than many school leaders do. Business organizations frequently have more discretionary resources available and are quicker and better able to reward talent and outstanding performance. Likewise, they are also much more swift and certain in dealing with employees who can't, don't, or won't perform up to expectations. Businesses make no bones about rewarding their best and weeding out the rest.

Schools, on the other hand, are typically more timid and tentative in dealing with extremes in staff performance. Business organizations are no-nonsense when it comes to productivity (or lack of it). Schools are more wishy-washy.

Some principals and superintendents put up with a lot of mediocrity (or worse), in part because schools pride themselves on having a kinder and gentler culture than most corporations do. But is it really kind to sentence people to continue indefinitely in a job for which they are obviously ill prepared and ill suited? Is it kind to subject kids to weak teachers? Is it kind to allow employees to go on thinking they are doing OK when everyone else around them knows they're not? Is kindness synonymous with dishonesty? Unfortunately, there are plenty of administrators who act as if the answer is "Yes" to all of these questions. But in their heart of hearts, they know it's baloney!

The truth is that in running either a business or a school, real kindness requires differentiation—treating people differently. Differentiation simply means treating people the way they deserve to be treated. When employees show you who they really are, believe them and act accordingly.

It is unfair to treat people all the same, because they are all different. Teachers know and apply this principle in the classroom every day. Why don't they (and their supervisors) realize that it applies to adults as well?

Treating individuals individually and differently is the only way to make them feel understood and to build a strong overall organization. Differentiation means facing up to extremes (e.g., giving star performers what they have earned and also-rans what their performance warrants). It's making merit count for something.

Applying the carrot and the stick as needed is an act of the kind of "tough love" that educators like to talk so much about. Sometimes principals and superintendents have to be tough and seemingly cruel to be fair and humane.

Tough love is refusing to compromise standards, be an enabler for problem behavior, waiver, waffle, weasel out, or walk on eggs. It rejects camouflaging positive and negative feelings. And it is not just blaming a substandard employee, but accepting some blame as well.

My favorite illustration of tough love is the following one-sided conversation by an unnamed entrepreneur as quoted by Buckingham and Coffman in *First, Break All the Rules:*

Come in, sit down, I love you, you're fired; I still love you. Now get a drink and let's talk this through.

That's tough love. Who says you can't confront a poor performing colleague without losing a friend?

Such straight talk is difficult for many school officials. Educators like to soft-pedal difficult issues and pussyfoot around touchy topics to avoid hurting anyone's feelings or making someone mad. Of course, it never works.

Most dictionaries define euphemism as the "act of substituting a mild, indirect, or vague term for one considered more harsh, blunt, or offensive." Based on this definition, school administrators are notorious euphemizers. That makes it difficult to practice differentiation.

For some principals and superintendents, differentiation is doubly difficult because it involves ranking people—sorting the A's from the B's and the C's and everyone below. School officials sort and label kids all the time, yet many balk at ranking staff members. ("No one likes to play God and rank people, especially the bottom 10 percent. Differentiation is a tough issue."—Jack Welch)

It's not that school leaders can't tell the difference between top performance and marginal output. They can. Even the custodian who sweeps the floor knows who the best and worst teachers are in your school. The kids know. The parents do, too. So, do you? But do you treat them any differently?

The education community seems inexplicably committed to treating all its own exactly alike. It starts with how people are paid. In most situations, a superior, world-class teacher receives identical compensation to that of the weakest, laziest, most inept teacher with the same training and years of experience. Try to explain that to any successful business owner in your community.

It's an uneducated way to operate the education enterprise. Failing to differentiate is an abdication of leadership. It occurs too often in schools. Don't let it happen on your watch.

Everyone in any organization deserves to know where they stand. That's why effective leaders accept the responsibility of ranking and rating subordinates and then telling them how they came out. They are rigorous, but not ruthless. They say what needs to be said—as clearly as possible, as soon as possible—and move on. Is that the way you treat your staff members? It should be. But many administrators don't.

With so many limitations and shortcomings, can the principles of differentiation and tough love really work with public school staff, particularly teachers? You bet. But they require a little tweaking.

For example, schools can't discipline, demote, or dismiss unsatisfactory employees as hastily and handily as businesses can. Unions, contract language, tenure laws, and hair-trigger litigators all work against differential treatment of staff members at the high and low end of the performance scale in schools.

Have you tried to discipline or fire a teacher lately? If so, how many depositions, hearings, arbitration rulings, and court sessions did it take? In some states, it is now almost as difficult to discharge a teacher as it is to get rid of a fungus infection under your big toenail. Maybe more difficult.

This doesn't mean that creative school leaders can't find ways to neutralize weak staff members, work around their weaknesses, and, sometimes, even nudge them out of the school or out of the profession entirely.

The first steps are to build a support system around poor performers, match them up with stronger partners, or find alternative roles for them within the organization.

If these efforts don't work (particularly in the case of flagrant violations), most districts have a formal process for progressive discipline, involving a hierarchy of enforcement measures ranging from oral and written reprimands to suspension (paid and unpaid) and ultimate dismissal. These procedures are in place for a reason. Use them when necessary.

For the worst failures or infractions, getting rid of the offender may be the only viable recourse. Short of legal termination action, sometimes it is possible to "counsel" the party out of the school and into a different line of work.

We've all heard of school leaders who have run out of other options and issue an ultimatum: "Resign or certain incriminating information will be made public." When it is explained that way, many people will choose to save face and avoid embarrassment by voluntarily removing themselves from the situation.

Of course, there are other pressures that school officials can employ to convince misfits to switch careers. I'm reminded of a secondary art instructor who was a bad teacher and a worse disciplinarian. She really hated teaching but liked the hours, the pay, and the benefits.

After repeated unsuccessful efforts to salvage the underperforming teacher, the principal asked himself, "Do I want this person on my school staff for the next 20 years?" The unequivocal answer was simply "no way." So the desperate principal decided to take some desperate measures.

Teaming with two supportive district administrators, the principal worked out a schedule of daily observations of the teacher's classroom performance. Each observation was documented in writing. The observers only recorded what transpired without editorializing. They didn't need to. The teacher's inadequate and inappropriate behavior was damaging enough without embellishment.

Despite cries of harassment, the observers kept up their daily visitations throughout the semester. After several months, the teacher decided it wasn't worth it and resigned.

She is now pursuing a successful art career and is admittedly happier with a life lacking in squirming teenagers. What she once viewed as harassment, she now appreciates as the best thing that ever happened to her.

You've got to love principals like the one in this example. The public schools will never have enough of them.

Contrary to what some educators think, working to remove the bottom 10 percent of performers from a school staff isn't cruel. What is cruel is allowing marginal employees to plug along year after year in a job they hate, feeling miserable, making all those around them equally miserable and shortchanging countless kids in the process.

That's not only cruel, it's inexcusable. Any principal or superintendent who hangs on to losers out of misguided loyalty, cowardice, or false kindness deserves to have to live with them—but the students and parents don't.

Obviously, school leaders can't do everything that their counterparts in business can do to deal with weak employees. But there is still plenty they can do to improve or remove unsatisfactory staff members. There is no reason or excuse not to try.

The following additional tips from veteran human resource specialists can make it even easier:

- Give lots of second chances. But be very stingy with third, fourth, and fifth chances.

- Give poor performers frequent one-on-one feedback.

- Be relentless in holding up the mirror to subpar employees. Try to get them to see themselves as others see them.

- Use straight talk with marginal staff members. Tell it like it is. Trying to find softer words does no one any favors.

- Offer help and support, not just criticism and penalties.

- Don't reward unsatisfactory behavior with an assignment to an easier, softer job. You might be surprised at how many of our largest school systems are currently carrying dozens of poor performing teachers and administrators who were unsuccessful in their original posts but are now reassigned to "made-up" jobs with phony titles where they can do a minimal amount of harm.

Some of the repositioned personnel actually like the arrangement—easy duty, no pressure, same pay, same benefits—what's not to like? Such subterfuges make a mockery of accountability and send the wrong message. No self-respecting business purposely carried dead wood on the payroll. No school should either.

• When dismissing personnel, do it as quickly as possible. Waiting always makes it worse.

Even with this advice, handling nonproductive employees is more difficult in the public sector. But "difficult" is the operable word. It's not the same as "impossible."

For principals and superintendents with a genuine urge to lead, the difficult is always doable; the impossible just takes a little longer.

Of course, just as schools cannot match everything businesses do to deal with poor performers, they also can't always reward their high flyers in the same way businesses do.

Schools aren't able to hand out salary increases, bonuses, or promotions to peak performers the way some corporations do. But there are lots of ways to "hug" your best people and let them know you love them, appreciate them, and want them to stick around.

If you can't reward your champions financially, concentrate on intangible rewards, such as pride, praise, and recognition. ("Talent thrives on thoughtful gestures, perks, and other signs of appreciation from management."—Mark McCormack, business columnist)

Faltering staff members demand a certain amount of attention, but successful leaders always focus most on their "keepers." It pays to overpay good people any way you can.

You don't have to be in a large school or a rich school to show appreciation to the heroes of the organization and to make them feel rewarded. Differential treatment of top performers doesn't always mean expensive treatment.

To make my case, here are a dozen ways to give superstars the special treatment they deserve—and all are well within the reach of any school:

1. Show your respect by asking your A+ staff members for advice. Even superstars are flattered and honored when their ideas and opinions are solicited by superiors.

2. Form a Creativity Council comprising your best people. Its only assignment: to brainstorm ways to move your school from good to great. It's an opportunity people are proud to receive.

3. Celebrate small successes by sounding a siren or ringing a bell to assemble the office staff for a one-minute standing ovation.

4. Put your best people to work on your most exciting projects, not just on your worst problems.

5. Show your willingness to deal with weak links. It makes your most productive employees feel that their efforts are not wasted.

6. Don't "de-motivate" peak performers by insulting them with transparent inducements or incentive programs. Superstars don't need motivating. They are self-starters. What they need is respect. Give it to them.

7. Make liberal use of "authentic praise" (real praise for real accomplishment). Be specific. Be timely. Be creative with your compliments (e.g., "Your idea is great. Sometimes I believe you can think through walls.")

8. Champion your best teachers and other staff members. Be their strongest advocate and cheerleader. Promote their careers even if it means losing them.

9. Keep your best people in the loop of insider information. Let them know they will always be the first to know important good and bad news within the organization. Knowledge makes people feel empowered.

10. Give selected top performers your cell phone number and permission to contact you at any time (even on weekends) with their ideas, questions, and suggestions.

11. Send copies of glowing performance reviews to the employee's spouse or significant other.

12. Do whatever it takes to make your top staff members feel that they are

> *asked, not questioned;*
> *measured, not monitored;*
> *people, not personnel;*
> *instrumental, not instruments;*
> *contributors, not costs;*
> *needed and heeded.*

—Jeffrey J. Fox (*How to Become CEO*)

Who says the best way to reward first-class employees is with big bucks? What high performers often want most are your time, your ear, your full attention, your respect, your loyalty, your support, and your praise.

You can be lavish with these rewards no matter what your budget is. Can you think of any reason not to be?

All school leaders want to be fair to both their top-end performers and their weaker staff members. The way to do it isn't by treating unequals equally. Rather, it is by differentiating—giving all parties what they need.

If you want to be the kind of leader your school deserves, you have to learn when to praise and when to prod, when to meddle (usually when you can make the greatest difference) and when to back off (usually when your intervention probably won't change anything anyway).

Leaders have to be like thermos bottles. (Now there's a comparison you probably never expected to see in print. But the analogy fits.) Some people think the lowly thermos is mankind's greatest invention because it keeps hot things hot and cold things cold. And it knows "when to which."

As it turns out, Jack Welch had it right. To succeed as a principal or superintendent today, you have to "kick butt and hug." And to make it even more challenging, you have to know when to which!

L Low-Maintenance Leadership

. . . to be simple is to be great.

—Ralph Waldo Emerson
transcendental writer and philosopher

Our schools no longer function primarily to teach . . . [Their] new role is best described as an amalgam of part surrogate parent, part chemical dependency clinic, part violence prevention shelter, part diversity trainer, part day-care center and part Drug Enforcement Administration. . . . The educational toad has so many social agenda warts it can no longer hop.

—Gary J. Gustafson
small business owner and former teacher

The only thing that saves us from bureaucracy is its inefficiency.

—Eugene McCarthy
former presidential candidate

Africans have a word for Westerners that literally translated means "people who spin." Are we running in circles and spinning out of control? Many people think so. And schools are not excluded from this assessment.

A 2001 study conducted by the Work Institute revealed that one third of American workers feel overworked and overwhelmed. (It may be even higher among school personnel.)

Most people now agree that life in the new millennium—at least in our society—has become a little too fast, too furious, and too complicated for comfort. It's that way in schools, too. If you don't agree, take another look at your calendar . . . and at your life.

Herein lies one of the best-kept secrets in school administration. (This would be a good time to get out your highlighter.)

What's needed most by today's (and tomorrow's) school leaders is the ability to bring simplicity, clarity, and focus to schools that are increasingly too big, too complicated, too fragmented, too impersonal, too costly, and too hard to change. "High-maintenance" schools are slow and inefficient and don't get the job done anymore.

It's like dating someone who is extremely "high maintenance"— someone who requires too much effort, too much time, too much attention, too much space, too much money, too much of everything. It's not worth it.

Unfortunately, school administrators themselves can be high maintenance. Like the bad date, high-maintenance administrators are usually more trouble than they are worth to the central office or the school board. They require too much care and feeding. They ask too many questions, make too many demands, and require too much hand-holding.

They constantly need to be noticed, validated, and propped up. They always need more budget, more staff, or more something. They're pests.

It doesn't take long for superiors to get tired of high-maintenance principals or superintendents. Soon no one higher up wants to see them coming, to meet with them, or even to return their phone calls.

I remember one administrator under my supervision who felt compelled to give me daily updates whether I needed them or not—in person, in my office—first thing every morning. He camped outside my office and pounced as soon as I arrived each day. He told me more than I wanted to know on subjects I didn't need to know about anyway. Eventually, I quit listening. Then I quit caring.

Being a high-maintenance nuisance is not a career-building strategy. If you really want to survive and thrive in the school leadership business, do your job, remain self-sufficient, run a low-maintenance organization, and make yourself indispensable to someone higher up.

And never hide behind a lack of resources. Instead, prove you can do more with less. That way, you will always be in demand.

Of course, there is one thing even worse than an individual high-maintenance administrator. It's a high-maintenance school—an entire school that is overly complicated, cumbersome, and costly. If that sounds like your school, it's time you learned some low-maintenance leadership skills.

It's no secret (or is it?) that there is more power in simplicity than in complexity. Simplicity is a leadership tool that can help school executives work smarter. Any principal or superintendent would be a fool not to use it.

The main forces contributing to confusion and complexity in today's schools are repetitious reforms, mushrooming bureaucracy, faulty communication, multiple missions, fuzzy goals, proliferating choices, and too much comfort with the status quo.

The best antidote is a low-maintenance environment featuring no artificial assignments, no useless red tape, no unnecessary or obligatory meetings, no mixed messages, no ambivalent goals, no overlapping authority, and no redundant layers of approval. That could be a blueprint for your school in the future.

Simplicity works because it is rooted in common sense. Simplifying an organization always enhances several important assets:

- *Problem solving:* the ability to resolve issues and keep them resolved.

- *Clarity:* a clear vision and mutual acceptance, support, and advocacy of school goals.

- *Creativity:* inventiveness, innovation, and risk taking.

- *Coping skills:* the capacity to respond to changing student needs while resisting irrelevant external demands.

If you want to run a better school, it's not that difficult—just simplify, simplify some more, and simplify all over again.

The first steps in low-maintenance leadership are to flatten the organizational structure as much as possible and "bust the bureaucracy" once and for all.

Start by dismantling any excessive administrative hierarchy. A multi-layered hierarchy implies that all the brains in the organization are at the top. You know as well as anyone that's not true.

Having too many generals (or assistants, associates, deputies, or deans) is as bad as not having enough foot soldiers. There should be a bounty for every extraneous administrative post and every layer of overlapping approval that is reduced or eliminated.

Too many layers slow down the organization, stifle creativity, and reinforce rigidity. If you need a metaphor, recall the old Charlie Brown comic strip in which Charlie is so bundled up for winter that he can hardly move, and if he topples over, he can't get up again. That's what too many layers will do for you.

Outside of education, many business organizations are becoming increasingly layerless and boundaryless. Many are moving toward a matrix organization with a flattened-out hierarchy. In these structures, horizontal organization is as important as vertical organization. Would that work in your school? Think about it. More and more schools are signing up.

When you are ready to create a low-maintenance organization, start by working backward from what teachers and other staff members need; move control closer to the department or classroom level and allow ideas to percolate from the bottom up. It will make yours a better school. And that makes you a better school leader, doesn't it?

In addition to compressing the hierarchy of decision making, it pays to root out all the other rudiments of bureaucracy (e.g., excessive paperwork, duplication of effort, layered channels of authority, or voluminous regulations).

And don't make the mistake of thinking that bureaucracy is a function of size. Small schools can be as role-bound and rule-bound as large ones.

The bottom line is that there just isn't much good to be said for bureaucracy in schools no matter what their size. But there is no end of justifiable criticism (e.g., "if bureaucracy is doing its job, it will, in effect, create roles, rules and structures that make the development of personalized, academic learning difficult, if not impossible."—Joseph Murphy)

The worst thing about bureaucracy is that it spreads incessantly. Bureaucracy is creepy. It creeps into every facet of the operation if you let it; eventually, it becomes all there is. ("Bureaucracy is the death of achievement." —Albert Einstein)

Fortunately, there are many steps that principals and superintendents can take to "bust the bureaucracy" in schools and create a lean, mean education machine. Here's a sampling of a few of the best low maintenance strategies:

• At regular intervals, walk through the school trying to see things through the eyes of the students and teachers. Look for what needs to be changed to enable them to work easier, better, faster, or smarter. Remember that removing obstacles is your number-one job.

• Don't require any monthly or quarterly written reports. If you get any, refuse to read them.

• Simplify school policies and rules. While serving as governor of Minnesota, Jesse Ventura suggested that the state legislature meet annually. On even-numbered years, it would pass needed legislation. But on odd years, it could only repeal obsolete, unnecessary, or unworkable laws and not pass anything new. It never happened in Minnesota, but maybe school boards should consider operating that way.

One of the first steps in low-maintenance leadership is to throw out the school's voluminous policy manual and ensure that all remaining policies serve students, not just adults.

Although business organizations are notorious for erecting monumental bureaucracies, some can actually serve as models in policy simplification. For instance, the policy manual for Sprint contains only two admonitions: come to work and wear clothes. Likewise, Nordstrom is famous for having only two rules: Number 1. Use good judgment in all situations. Number 2. There will be no additional rules.

Not to be outdone, Continental Airlines replaced its traditional policy manual with an abbreviated set of "Working Together Guidelines." Can your school match or top that?

Besides scaling back the policy manual, low-maintenance schools allow staff members to deviate from standard policy when the situation warrants (e.g., waiving zero-tolerance rules in extenuating circumstances).

Sometimes rule breaking is more important than rule making. ("Any fool can make a rule."—Henry David Thoreau) You can't go wrong giving your teachers and other employees permission to solve problems without waiting for front office approval.

• Change the rules when necessary so that everyone on staff can do what matters.

• Spend more time and money on people than on technology. If you hire good people and treat them as adults, you won't need a lot of rules and checkpoints.

• Assign budgets to projects or programs rather than allocating blanket amounts to departments.

• When needed, bypass established channels and deal directly with other high-ranking leaders. Bureaucracies usually move at a glacial pace because there is a bureaucrat waiting at each level to hold things up. Navigating layers of approval takes time. Sometimes it is only the top administrators who have the clout to cut through obstacles, objections, and red tape to create momentum and to get things done.

• Eliminate clutter (both physical and mental) so employees can get their work done and still have time to think.

• Have a Dinosaur stamp made to use in marking extinct or outdated reports or ideas. It worked for Mike Warren, president of Alagasco in Birmingham, Alabama.

• Cross-train employees. Require nonteaching personnel to learn each other's jobs. It will allow you to cover absences and handle overtime with fewer extra people. Best of all, trading jobs promotes fresh perspectives that can uncover overlooked shortcuts.

• Make informal conversations count. Use "face time" with colleagues at all levels to get things done. Little conversations are better than rules, and small talk can lead to big changes. Most confusion, problems, and misunderstandings in schools occur because of conversations that never took place.

The whole purpose of these and other low-maintenance measures is to make it easier for the system to work and easier to work the system. They are your best insurance against becoming a high-maintenance administrator or running a high-maintenance school.

The final word is this: If you want to distinguish yourself as a principal or superintendent in our increasingly complicated world, you have to master the fine art of simplification.

Unfortunately, making things simple is hard work. ("Finding a way to live the simple life today is man's most complicated task."—Henry A. Courtney)

Nobody ever said that low-maintenance leadership is easy, but it is simply what works best today.

 Metaphors
and Morale

Morale is faith in the man at the top.

—Albert S. Johnstone

. . . the morale of an organization is not built from the bottom up, it flows from the top down.

—Peter B. Kyne

When was the last time you thought seriously about the morale of the people working in your school (other than your own)? If you are like many school officials, it was too long ago.

We don't hear much about morale anymore. It's too bad, because morale is still a critical determiner of success for every kind of organization.

How people feel about their job, their work environment, and their boss shapes how they perform. You can't have high performance and low morale at the same time. (That's one note you can write in ink.)

When people feel crummy about their job, they do a crummy job. When everyone, from the top to the bottom of the organization, feels satisfied, challenged, excited, and fulfilled by their work—look out world—great things are going to happen. It's called high morale. And it's as true in your school as anywhere.

What does this morale stuff have to do with school leadership? Everything! Morale is contagious. People "catch it" from their leaders. High morale is always the result of successful leadership.

Unfortunately, too many principals and superintendents don't pay enough attention and don't do enough to boost and maintain staff morale—partly because they assume it's expensive (who has a budget for morale?). They're wrong. Actually, good morale comes cheap.

Leaders create and influence morale largely by what they say and do, not by how much they spend on it. It starts with the words they choose to describe and explain their organization.

Words set a tone. They are mood makers and mood breakers. They evoke emotions, trigger memories, and generate visceral reactions. They build bridges between leaders and followers—or they burn them. As the leader, how you talk about the school affects how the people in it perceive and feel about it.

As an example, if you are like most principals and superintendents, you frequently call on descriptive metaphors to get your message across because they are catchy, interesting, and colorful. Listen to yourself for a while. You may be surprised and amazed at how much you rely on comparisons to communicate with your many audiences.

Metaphors are popular because they can simplify complex issues, focus attention, teach a lesson, define problems, help find solutions, and make your vision stand out from the crowd. Metaphors allow people to see things in a new way.

Metaphors can inform, instruct, and inspire. ("Metaphors can be great motivational tools because they are easy to understand and hard to forget."—Dave Yoffie, author of *Judo Strategy*) They can do all that—but only if they fit the situation.

A good metaphor makes sense out of confusion. A bad metaphor only creates confusion where good sense once prevailed.

The problem is that too many school leaders use inaccurate or inappropriate metaphors. The results are mixed messages, false perceptions, faulty conclusions, and sometimes diminished morale.

The power of metaphors was forcefully brought home to me several years ago while working for a superintendent new to the district.

During his first few months on the job, he seemed to do all the right things. He was visible and accessible. He listened. He preached family values and tried to live by his principles. He was upbeat and quickly became a cheerleader for the school and the staff. Yet acceptance was slow in coming.

Veteran staff members remained skeptical, guarded, and on edge. Employees, at all levels, felt stressed without knowing why. Morale was sinking. Something was wrong; but no one could pinpoint the problem.

Finally, an outside consultant unraveled the mystery. The superintendent was in the habit of using military metaphors and references when talking about the organization. His speech was riddled with phrases such as, "take no prisoners" and "our first line of defense." As it turns out, it was his language, not his behavior, that was distancing colleagues and coworkers.

He was using the wrong metaphors for an institution that relies on good will, cooperation, and teamwork for success. Once he stopped using military comparisons, his acceptance and approval ratings improved immediately. Metaphors matter.

As you listen to yourself and others, how often do you hear the same mistake as that made by my misguided new superintendent? Scary, isn't it?

Military comparisons create a military mentality. Like sports metaphors, they may work in a highly competitive situation, such as business; they do not work for schools.

Warlike words and references (see examples) invoke a warlike mindset in which someone has to win and someone has to lose. Education isn't a war. There aren't supposed to be any losers. No one has to die.

Teachers and other school staff members don't want to be soldiers. They don't view students as the enemy. They see what they do as collaborative, not combative. Military metaphors make them uncomfortable and unsure of their mission. Military references are bad for morale in schools. It's that simple. Don't use them. Ever.

The Language of Military Metaphors

Front lines	Good soldiers	Bring out the
In the trenches	Take cover	big guns
Battles	Marching orders	Minefield
Weapons	Bombard	Booby trap
Attack	Unconditional	Guard the fort
Troops	surrender	Enemy lines
Surrender	Surprise attacks	Blitzkrieg
Combat Zone	Guerrilla warfare	Man your guns
Under fire	Fire power	To the victor go
Ammunition	Divide and conquer	the spoils
Battle scars	Man the battle	Lose the battle
Charge!	stations	and win the war
		Under fire

Do you use these terms? Do they fit what your school is all about? Think about it.

Luckily, there are many better choices (see examples). The point is to choose and use words, descriptors, and metaphors that capture the positive aspects of teaching and learning (e.g., creativity, synergy, interdependence, and joy). Selecting the right reference, comparison, or analogy doesn't cost any more, but choosing the wrong metaphor can be costly.

Metaphors That Work for Schools

- Nature: ecosystem, rebirth, cycles
- Music: conductor, orchestrate, harmony, change of tempo, improvisation
- Birds: eagles, doves
- Gardens: planting seeds, nurturing
- Martial arts studio (*dojo*): place to be your best, compete with yourself, respect, discipline, standards

---

Of course, it takes more than words to build and sustain high morale among all school staff members. It takes action, too. But one thing it doesn't take is a lot of money.

Morale isn't a function of economics. It's a function of leadership. You can have high morale in the poorest of schools and low morale in a wealthy school. It seems almost too good to be true, but morale isn't a matter of money. It's mostly a matter of leaders treating people right.

A classic case in point is the simple act of recognition. If you don't know that the desire for recognition and appreciation is universal, you've been holed up in your office too long. ("The deepest principle of human nature is the craving to be appreciated."—William James, psychologist)

David Boyle, author of *The Sum of Our Discontent*, reports that a few years ago, the Midland Banks of England invested $6.5 million on employee incentive programs, only to discover that workers just want someone to come by and say, "Good job," now and then. (Bank employees and school personnel must have a lot in common.)

The Midland experience was no fluke. Repeated studies have shown that employees in all fields find personal recognition more motivating than money. ("There are two things people want more than sex and money . . . recognition and praise."—Mary Kay Ash) This is good news for most schools (maybe yours included) that are chronically strapped for funds.

It doesn't cost anything to show appreciation to the people who work in your school, to acknowledge their contributions and accomplishments, and to recognize them as individuals. But it can pay back big dividends in staff morale.

Don't buy into the conventional wisdom that holds that people should not be recognized just for doing their job—after all, that's what they are hired and paid to do. Balderdash! That's exactly why they should be recognized.

To be most effective, informal recognition (e.g., a thank you note or pat on the back) should be given to every employee almost weekly and more formal recognition (such as a special award) less frequently. Formal recognition should take place in a public ceremony whenever possible to give it symbolic importance and meaning beyond its actual worth.

Recognizing associates is easy. It's free (or at least inexpensive), and it works. High morale depends on it. If you are not already doing everything you can think of to show your teachers and support personnel that they are appreciated, the time to begin is now.

If you need help getting started, following are 33 of the best no-cost and low-cost ways to recognize staff members, to show appreciation, to jump-start flagging morale, or to push existing high morale further off the charts. These ideas come from some of the best businesses and schools in the country. (There is no extra charge for this service.)

1. Pick up the nominal membership fee for your key clerical personnel to join Professional Secretaries International (PSI). It will validate their professionalism and probably upgrade their skills at the same time.

2. Hold an in-house parade to honor staff members who have made singular contributions.

3. Have your parent organization supply free popcorn and apples in the teachers' lounge every day.

4. Allow school staff members to take adult community education classes free of charge.

5. Send a "Bravo Card" when appropriate.

6. Sell take-home dinners in the cafeteria after school. The moms on your payroll will love it.

7. Give all teachers' kids free passes to high school sporting events. The Lawrence (Kansas) Public Schools have issued "T.K. Passes" for years.

8. Let staff members with large families use school facilities for reunions and holiday gatherings at no charge.

9. Include the achievements of employees' children in your school newsletter.

10. Many schools issue bumper stickers for "proud parents." Why not hand out stickers for proud teachers and other staff members?

11. Arrange for free at-school shoe shines or parking lot car washes and oil changes for staff members during the school day.

12. Host a campout on the school playground for staff members and their families.

13. Arrange for special talent (e.g., mimes, jugglers, magicians, barber shop quartets, etc.) to entertain your staff after school. Many individuals and groups will perform free of charge for teachers.

14. Make no-charge family photo sessions available at school for staff members at holiday time.

15. Take a tip from Bill Nesbit, Central Telephone Company of Illinois, by giving outstanding employees a lottery ticket with an accompanying note, "I never gamble when I count on you."

16. Instead of giving an employee a dozen flowers on a special occasion, try having one flower per hour delivered throughout an entire day. That takes making someone feel special to a whole new level.

17. Keep a supply of free greeting cards on hand for employee use.

18. Set up a quiet room where frustrated teachers and other staff members can scream and pound on the walls. It works at the Levi Straus Company.

19. Adopt the principle of "blameless errors" to remove employee fear of failure.

20. Create special employee awards (they don't have to be expensive), such as a Behind-the-Scenes Award, and ABCD (Above and Beyond the Call of Duty) Award or an IgNoble Award patterned after those granted by the *Annals of Improbable Research,* a journal devoted to zany, stupid, and useless research studies.

21. Send "I'm in your corner" notes of encouragement.

22. Arrange for volunteer parents to provide concierge services to help teachers and other staffers with personal business and errands.

23. Allow special teachers to ride separately in a limo when accompanying or chaperoning a school field trip. Sandburg Middle School in Anoka, Minnesota, has done this for retiring teachers.

24. Arrange for at-school pickup and delivery of dry cleaning.

25. "Rehire" your best performers. Make it a point to tell them how good they are.

26. Get qualified parents to volunteer as personal coaches or trainers for interested staff members.

27. Set aside a regular time for the spouses and families of staff members to ask questions and air gripes about the school. It always pays to remember the families of employees.

28. Allow staff members to bring their own children to the school cafeteria for lunch on special occasions. Be sure to provide enough high chairs and booster seats.

29. Persuade a local bank to offer low-range mortgage rates for teachers.

30. Provide "workplace chaplains" (e.g., volunteer religious counselors, rabbis, priests, and ministers) to help meet employee spiritual needs.

31. Reward high-performing staff members with gift certificates under $25. That way, the employee won't incur any extra tax burden. One company calls them "De minimus awards."

32. Arrange for teachers to get a price break from local child-care providers.

33. Try to negotiate a "broadband" pay plan with broad, overlapping bands (ranges) of pay for each role. Under such plans, a super-star teacher may be more highly compensated than a novice, untested principal. Wow! Now, that's recognition.

Of course, these suggestions are just a starter set. There is no end of creative ways to help school staffs feel valued and keep them thrilled about their work.

You can't do them all. You don't have to. But you do need to make a continuing, concentrated, and conscious effort to notice what people are doing, recognize their progress and productivity, and treat them right.

Unfortunately, when it comes to morale building, some principals and superintendents follow the DALAP principal—Do As Little As Possible. And it shows.

Whenever you find low morale in any school, don't look to the budget, the state of the building, the kids, or any other working condition. Look to the leader.

Real leaders take care of their people, so that their people will take care of them and take care of business. It's win–win. Leaders don't "get" people to do the right thing. They create an environment where everyone wants to do the right thing and wants to do it right.

High morale has to be choreographed. After all, managing morale in your school is a dance—and you get to lead! (I told you educators can't resist a good metaphor.)

Networking and Nit-Picking

The employer usually gets the employees he deserves.

—Sir Walter Bilbey

Without bright, bold employees an organization quickly becomes tomorrow's road kill.

—Harris and Brannick
Finding and Keeping Great Employees

A mentor can tell you things you didn't learn in school.

—Sheila Wellington
businesswoman

Fussbudgets make lousy leaders. Authentic leaders don't have time to nitpick over trivial, petty, insignificant, or irrelevant details. They're too busy and have more important things to do. So they usually just follow acclaimed author Richard Carlson's highly publicized advice: "Don't sweat the small stuff."

But there is one thing that successful leaders in all fields are universally picky, choosy, and fussy about: people—the people with whom they associate, the people they hire, and the people they choose as mentors and as part of their professional support network.

Leadership is all about people. Leaders don't lead technology or machines or money. They lead people. That's why good leaders surround themselves with good people—often people who are better than they are.

As a principal or superintendent you can be only as successful as the people around you, who work for and with you every day. One of the great cautions every leader who lasts pays attention to is this: Be very picky about the people you hang out with, the people you hire, the people you keep, and the people you pattern your career after. Are you paying attention? ("People are not your greatest asset. The *right* people are."—Jim Carlson)

It starts with the people you spend time with, on and off the job. Believe it or not, a great deal of your success depends on the company you keep. Winners spend time with winners. You can't learn excellence rubbing elbows with mediocrity.

Look around at how your heroes in the profession spend their time. They spend most of it with their best people, because talent expands when you invest time in it.

Conversely, your role models don't spend much time on ROAD Warriors (a military term for slackers who are "Retired on Active Duty") or too much time working on the weaknesses of weak performers. Neither should you.

The only people in any organization who are ever going to become truly outstanding at what they do are already damned good at it to start with. Working with them is the best use of a leader's time. Healthy organizations are built on strong bonds between good leaders and their best employees.

Some school administrators you know devote too much of their time to working with their weakest staff members in hopes of salvaging them or of engineering a metamorphosis from tailender to top performer. It doesn't work.

Miracles happen. But not often in your lifetime. It's rare that a leader can profoundly alter the basic nature of another adult.

In most situations, you have to work with what's there. If there isn't much there to start with, don't work at it very hard. ("Don't waste time trying to put in what was left out. Try to draw out what was left in. This is hard enough."—Marc Buckingham)

To make matters worse, while leaders are spending time with weak links, super stars may fizzle, get bored, or burn out from lack of attention. That makes it both a waste of time and of talent. It's a mistake you can't afford to make.

Of course, the only way to ensure that you always spend time with quality people is to hire only the best in the first place. And then keep them.

Hiring personnel is the hands-down, single most important decision any leader ever makes. There isn't any close second. This is one thing you absolutely have to get right. Your future (and your school's) depends on it.

Casting is everything. Hollywood producers know it. So do business headhunters. So should you.

In his best-seller, *Good to Great*, Jim Collins's first and most important bit of advice to business leaders is to "get the right people on the bus and the wrong people off the bus." Then you can decide where to go. When, how far, and how fast.

The bottom line is that every job is important, so be very picky—almost nitpicky—about the person you select for every position in the organization from top to bottom. Even one misfit assistant cook, floor sweeper, or substitute aide can cause you grief beyond belief.

One of the greatest contributions you can make to your school is to choose the right people, slot them into the optimum situation, and trust them to do the job. If you do this, being a principal or superintendent can be a dream job. If you don't, plan on a lot of nightmares.

One of the secrets of selecting a world-class staff is to look for what human resource directors in the business world call "hi-po"—high potential, not just training, skills, or experience. At Microsoft, they claim to hire for only one thing: "smarts." Can you think of any reason why you should settle for less? Hire people with mental firepower. You don't have to be a wealthy school to be rich in intellectual capital.

Besides intelligence, look for passion, character, and values. You won't find these things on a transcript or in a packet of credentials. That's what interviews, auditions, visitations, and background checks are for. Learn to look for the lies in an applicant's eyes.

A huge mistake many administrators make is to hire people just like themselves. Inbreeding is bad for families and just as unhealthy for organizations. You're better off with a heterogeneous staff that includes a good number of generalists.

Don't hire "plastic people" just because they are easy to manage and manipulate. Go after some pot-stirrers and cage-rattlers. Let it be known that talented mavericks are welcome on your staff. Be willing to put up with some abrasive staff members if they are also A+ performers in their job.

If you want a blueprint for staffing, you can't do much better than following Southwest Airlines' approach to personnel policy:

1. Be the best *you* possible.

2. We don't want clones.

3. Everyone is expected to color outside the lines.

The point is to be rigorous and relentless in going after the best. Don't settle. If you can't find what you're looking for, keep looking. Never be afraid to leave a position open for a while or to start your search all over again. The best school systems do it all the time.

Champion performers don't flock. You have to find them one by one. And they won't come to you. You have to be creative in going after them. Here are some insider tips that can make it easier for you to build and retain your own dream team for your school:

You never know where or when you are going to find just the person you're looking for, so always be on the lookout. Pay attention. Every chance encounter is a potential interview. Searching for the best teacher (or clerk or custodian) is something you should do 24 hours a day. It's what your competition is doing. Why give them an edge?

• Use a "council of many" in the staffing process. Never permit just one person to make any hiring decision. Involve as many good minds as you can.

It pays to have your A+ people help find more A+ people. Talent attracts talent. Solicit referrals from current staff members, and use your best teachers as campus recruiters.

Every new hire affects the entire school, so as much of the school staff as feasible should help pick new people. When current staff members have a hand in hiring, they also have a greater stake in seeing to it that newcomers succeed.

• You need some talented new teachers on your staff every year. There aren't that many of them, and every school wants them. They may not come to you, so be aggressive in going after them. Conduct your own Star Search. Get there first and beat the competition.

Be creative in enticing the best newcomers to join your team. The Cisco Company has been known to send pizzas to college residence halls during final exam week with a good luck note and an application form. What fresh recruitment ideas can you come up with?

• Keep in frequent touch with promising prospects via e-mail and phone contact. Too many candidates feel forgotten and abandoned while their application is under review. Let applicants know where they stand. If you don't want them, say so. But if you are still interested, let them know that, too.

• Use holidays to recruit former students home for vacation. Many "hi-po" prospects would jump at the chance to teach in their alma mater. Who says you can't go home again?

• Make it easy for newcomers to join your team:

a. Minimize paperwork and red tape.
b. Give signing bonuses and moving allowances when possible.

    c. Recruit volunteer students to help with the heavy lifting during the moving process.

    d. Help spouses with their job search.

    e. Arrange for new hires to shop for housing electronically.

• Pay attention to body language during job interviews. (Here's a clue veteran interviewers know about: Most candidates look left when they are creating a response—lying—and look right when they are just trying to remember something.)

• The last question you should always ask yourself before hiring any teacher is, "Would I want my child (or grandchild) to have this person for a whole year?"

Obviously, finding, attracting, and hiring outstanding people is hard work. But it's only half the battle. Keeping them is just as important and can be just as difficult.

Most experts agree that the following 10 steps are the most effective ways to keep your best employees:

    1. Find the right slot. ("If you want to turn talent into performance, you have to position so that you are paying her to do what she is naturally wired to do. Cast her in the right role."—Buckingham and Coffman, *First, Break All The Rules*)

    2. Define clear, reasonable expectations.

    3. Provide the necessary resources to do the job.

    4. Make success easy. (Remove obstacles.)

    5. Give authentic praise.

    6. Show appreciation. ("Too often, we find companies throwing money at a person to get them to stay. . . . That's not what's missing—it's feeling appreciated."—Chester Elton, Coauthor of *Managing With Carrots*)

    7. Treat all employees as individuals.

    8. Listen. Most employees would trade a year's vacation for a boss who really listens—and hears.

    9. Surround staff members at all levels with talented coworkers.

    10. Demonstrate an unflagging commitment to excellence.

Every time you hire and keep a top-notch performer, your life as a leader gets a little bit easier. That's why it pays to be picky.

But it's not just the people you work with that you should choose with care. It's equally important to be selective about the people you network with. And you had better be networking with someone. A good network is an essential life-support system for every school leader today.

A network is simply a professional support group that offers encouragement and a sympathetic ear. It is the newest professional growth strategy. And thanks to modern electronics, it can now include colleagues, counterparts, mentors and advisors from across the street and around the world.

Access to like-minded school administrators, who speak the same language and share common experiences and feelings, have become a critical resource for success for all school leaders. A well-rounded network is just another survival tool you can't afford to be without.

It's always lonely at the top. Sometimes it's even more lonely in the middle. As a superintendent or principal, you stand alone in your immediate organization. Being isolated can be scary. That's another good reason why you and every other school and business leader must develop a solid network of peers and mentors.

My favorite example of the power of support networks is the story of K.F., a recovering alcoholic who was suddenly faced with both divorce and unemployment. Sitting alone one day brooding at the sorry state of his life, he stared at the bottle of liquor in front of him and couldn't think of one good reason why he shouldn't start drinking again.

In one last effort to reach out for help, he pulled out the phone list from his local Alcoholics Anonymous (AA) group and started down the roster calling each member.

No one answered his first call, so he left a message. The second call produced the same result. As did the third. Eventually, he completed the entire list without reaching a single person in his support network.

K.F. took it as a sign. Feeling helpless and hopeless, he reached for the bottle. Just then, the phone rang. It was the first person he had called responding to his message. While talking to the caller, another call came in. And later, another. And another.

It continued, until at the end of the day, every person on his list had returned his call offering help, encouragement, and support. K.F. didn't drink that day. Or any other day. His support group was there when needed and turned his life around in a time of dire despair.

The story of K.F. isn't just an AA story. It's a network story. If you think that many successful school leaders haven't had similar career-saving experiences with networks, you're ill informed. It happens every day.

I've seen networks work, and I've seen them fail. I distinctly remember sitting in a meeting of suburban superintendents several years ago, while one of the group chastised the others for abandoning him during a protracted and bitter teacher strike.

Throughout the strike, none of his colleagues contacted him to offer support. Most were also slow to return his phone calls and avoided other contacts with him wherever possible. His closest "comrades in arms" were no longer available to him.

The beleaguered superintendent reported that he felt very much alone—like a leper leader—until the strike was settled. His network had failed him.

To this day, whenever a colleague is involved with any kind of strike or serious labor dispute, I make it a point to call or reach out in some way to offer encouragement and empathy. If you want to receive the support of a professional network, do your share of supporting in return.

Of course, it doesn't take a desperate situation, such as a strike, to realize the benefits of networking. A good support network helps with everyday stuff as well.

There are times when all leaders need to interact with others who understand their situation, who know firsthand what they are going through and who can give honest feedback based on real-world experience. What you can't ask your boss or your subordinates, you can always ask your network.

A carefully chosen network extends your knowledge and multiplies your wisdom and experience. Obviously, the benefits of networking are many and varied including opportunities to

- Exchange information and ideas.
- Engage in collaborative problem solving.
- Seek support and encouragement.
- Vent frustration.
- Gain perspective.
- Get a reality check.
- Philosophize.
- Brainstorm alternatives.
- Ask "what do you do about" questions.
- Get advice.
- Gain moral support.
- Find examples.
- Solicit suggestions.
- Get feedback.
- Explore alternative scenarios.
- See the humor in stressful situations.
- Get a second opinion.

- Swap "war stories."
- Let your hair down and have fun.

So if you think you can get along without a strong network, you're out of touch with reality. You don't even know what you don't know. When you are not in a network of caring colleagues, you're missing out on a valuable, built-in fan club and advisory council.

Take my word for it. You need a network—now! No one has a monopoly on wisdom, and no one is too big to need help now and then.

Unfortunately, it is sometimes difficult for women administrators—particularly women of color—to find a suitable network. There are, however, several successful models in both the business world and in education, such as the "Synniken Sisters."

Synniken is a Greek word for "winning together." In Minneapolis, 10 successful women executives, calling themselves the Synniken Sisters, formed their own version of an "old boys' club" to pool their experience and knowledge to help their careers. Over the years, the group has taken networking to the next level; members now offer support to each other in areas well beyond the job.

As an example of a broader scale effort, Northwestern Mutual Life Insurance Company has initiated a "Circle of Success" program featuring support groups to help recruit and retain female workers. The program includes mentorships, discussion guides, and meetings to help women figure on how best to support one another. Would something like this work in your school system?

If you can't find similar networks in your situation, start your own. Do whatever it takes to establish a viable network that meets your needs. This isn't just something that it would be nice to do. This is something you absolutely have to do to survive and thrive as a school leader today.

The good news is that in most cases, it's not hard to network. If you are open to networking, you will find a network open to you. Best of all, networking is a moveable feast that can expand, contract, or adapt to meet your changing needs.

Your professional network can either lift you up or let you down. It all depends on the people in it. Choose carefully. Naturally, you want only the most talented, experienced and sensible people available. And be sure to include one or two seasoned mentors in the group. An administrator without a mentor is like a student without a teacher.

Mentoring occurs in all fields. Business executives have mentors. So do doctors and lawyers. And so should you. A good mentor is a guide, a coach and an advocate who can teach you all the informal rules of success in your field.

The experience of many of your fellow administrators suggests that to get the most from any mentoring relationship, you should follow three simple rules:

1. Be strategic. Know what you need to learn and match with a mentor who can teach it to you.

2. Respect your mentor's time.

3. Have a plan for divorcing your mentor when appropriate or if the relationship doesn't work out.

Some principals and superintendents ratchet the concept of mentoring up a notch by hiring a personal coach. It's something to consider.

Personal coaches are hired to help clients define and prioritize goals and values, identify what needs changing in their lives, develop an action plan, and keep them on track.

Coaches instruct, inspire, and motivate, but they don't perform therapy. It's the client, however, who has to do all the real work.

Most coaching sessions are conducted over the phone for about a half hour each week. It's a small commitment if it changes your life or career for the better.

Personal coaching is so effective that some companies, such as financial services giant ING, hire coaches to work with their managers. Some schools have also experimented with providing coaches for administrators.

The Minneapolis Public Schools have used business volunteers from IBM and other corporations to work with principals on management. The business coaches help school leaders shape strategies, think through issues, and make decisions that improve process and performance.

Besides helping the school officials, the program also gives their business counterparts a new appreciation of what school leaders really do. As one volunteer business coach reported, "The work of an inner-city principal is tough, perhaps more complicated than that of many corporate managers."

Whether it's a personal coach, a mentor or members of a professional network, you need others to help you master the leadership game. But not just anybody will do. You need the right people on the bus.

There are many people in your life. Most of them are there because of some action you have taken. If the people with whom you associate, work, and network are not supporting, challenging, and helping you grow, it's your fault. You picked the wrong people.

The people around you are your competitive edge. It's OK to be picky about them. In fact, it's a prerequisite for successful leadership in any field.

As a leader, you achieve results only through others. People are your tools. Like all tools, if you choose them carefully, stick with the best, take good care of them, and keep them sharp, they will get the job done.

Don't worry too much about yourself. Worry about and care for the people around you. And they will propel you to the top. If you don't believe me, ask your network.

O Optimism or Else

Medical studies now make it official. Optimists do better. People with a positive attitude and outlook live longer and feel better in the process. It should come as no surprise, then, that optimists also succeed as leaders more often than pessimists.

How you view life, kids, and the future helps determine how well you do as a principal or superintendent. Your bias about people can also have a lot to do with your success and effectiveness.

Business leaders have known this for a long time. Ken Fracaro makes the case, "An optimistic attitude is an essential characteristic for a supervisor/manager to possess in order to attain goals, increase productivity, motivate employees and accept change."

In business and in school leadership, optimists have an edge over pessimists. You see it happen every day, because pessimism is a self-fulfilling prophecy.

Whether it's in a corporate boardroom, a school boardroom, or a classroom, pessimists are their own worst enemies. They expect the worst. They predict the worst. They prepare for the worst. They plan on it. And the worst often happens to them. Life tends to live down to their expectations.

It may not be fair, but pessimists bring most of their troubles on themselves through their own self-defeating behaviors. They self-destruct in many ways:

- Their negative attitude chases away those people who could support and help them most.
- They can't separate malicious attacks from constructive criticism.
- They are easily distracted, because they are always looking for signs of failure. (To the pessimist, any bump in the road looks like the end of the road.)
- Pessimists are more prone to panic and paranoia.
- They are overly self-critical.
- They often worry themselves into illness.
- Worse yet, they give up too soon.

It's no wonder that pessimists make lousy leaders. Of course, some people will follow a persuasive pessimist anyway, but there is no joy in the journey when the only destination is doom and gloom.

For most people, bad luck is random. For pessimists, it's a given. They create their own misfortunes. Optimists, however, operate just the opposite. They create their own breaks by focusing on successes, salvaging what they can from failures, seeing problems as opportunities for triumph, taking a long view, refusing to personalize mistakes, and simply sticking to it.

Being optimistic doesn't mean school leaders are Pollyannas. (There's a difference between hope and delusion.) Most are realistic in accepting that problems, setbacks, troubles, and even tragedies happen—periodically. They refuse, however, to allow reversals to prevail. This way they create their own scenarios for success. If you believe in happy endings, you are more likely to experience them.

Look at the principals and superintendents you know and respect. How many naysayers and doom dealers are there? None is the right answer. All successful school leaders have an optimistic attitude. They have to. It gives them an edge that you can have, too.

The obvious benefits of optimism are substantial, including less stress, more confidence, better use of time, greater satisfaction, reduced burnout; and greater openness to opportunity and risk taking.

An optimistic view of the world can set your school apart. It can distance you from the increasing number of school officials and faculties who are constantly whining and bemoaning bad times for education.

Internationally recognized management expert Tom Peters stresses that successful organizations need a "WOW factor" that allows them to step out and stand out "from the growing crowds of look-alikes." A passionate "optimism or else" attitude can become the "WOW factor" that propels your school ahead of the pack.

Best of all, optimism can enable you and your school to do more— maybe even to do the impossible. The World War II motto of the U.S. Army Services was "The difficult we do immediately. The impossible takes a little longer." That could be the motto of your school as well. With optimism like that, how can you fail?

Optimism has the power to uplift the spirit and energize the soul of your school. But can just anyone tap into that power? Can you develop a more optimistic attitude if you want to? Can you improve your chances of success as a school leader by intentionally becoming more positive in your outlook? A good optimist always says, "Yes—positively!"

Pessimism is a prison that some educators impose on themselves. You know administrators whose negative attitude locks them into a pattern of failure. It doesn't have to be that way. Attitudes and outlooks can change. It's called growth.

Of course, no one can be 100 percent positive, 100 percent of the time. Good school leaders are optimistic, not terminally perky.

There are times when everyone's optimism needs a second wind. So whenever you positively need to boost your optimism quotient, try the following attitude adjusters (If they don't make you feel hopeful, nothing will):

1. Stay healthy. A healthy body is a precursor for a healthy attitude.

2. Don't try to remain too "cool." Dare to be enthusiastic. Let it show. It will pump you up, catch on with others, and improve your chances for success.

3. Watch your posture. Stand and walk erect. You just feel more positive and powerful when you "stand tall."

4. Use positive affirmations to talk yourself into a positive frame of mind.

5. Remember the good times in the bad times.

6. Listen to upbeat music. They call it "mood music" for a reason.

7. Look for what's right about your job and your school.

8. Spend time with positive people.

9. Visualize the best.

10. Make a big deal out of what's working in your school. Celebrate victories great and small.

11. Avoid "sour grapes" and look for the "sweet lemons" instead. Make something good out of bad news. In times of retrenchment, don't dwell on the layoffs; focus on the "keepers."

12. Stand up to the pessimists and crepe-hangers on your staff and in your community. When Dr. Owen Henson of Emporia State University encounters senior citizens lamenting the sorry condition of today's youth, he always counters by asking, "How are your grandkids doing?" Suddenly, the conversation takes a 180-degree turn.

13. Smile for no reason and laugh and play every day.

14. Be your own best friend. Pamper yourself. It's permitted—even for school administrators.

15. Live a balanced life. Make time for what's important. (Hint: Not all of it has anything to do with schools.)

16. Beware of Wednesdays. It's "hump day," when everyone needs a little midweek boost.

17. Do something nice for others. It's a surefire morale booster.

18. Believe in your staff and show it. You will convince them everything is going to be OK and convince yourself at the same time.

How about giving out safety pins as a symbol of support (a low-budget guardian angel) for staff members going through tough times? It works for an Alanon group in Nashville. It can work in your school as well.

Marcus Buckingham and Curt Coffman, coauthors of the business best-seller *First, Break All the Rules,* advocate sending staff positive memos and personal messages such as, "You are the best the school has and the best I have ever had the privilege to work with."

Whatever you can do to boost your staff will lift you at the same time.

19. Try holding a "Great American Grump Out Day" in your school where no one is allowed to bitch, whine, or complain. Similar to the National Smoke Out Day for quitting tobacco use, the idea was started by Janice Hathby in Kalamazoo, Michigan. It's catching on. It's good for families, businesses, schools, and entire communities.

20. Stay away from the curmudgeons and vultures who congregate in the teachers' lounge to complain about kids, parents, and life in general. Cynics can only drain your energy. They never contribute anything constructive.

21. If all else fails, go to the source—children. Visit a nursery for newborns. Hold a baby. Talk to a kindergartner on the first day of school.

Feel the love in a special education classroom. Attend a Bar Mitzvah. Go to a graduation (especially a GED [general education diploma] ceremony). Look in the eyes of a graduating senior.

All of these are signs telling you it's worth it. Who could be pessimistic or cynical after all that?

If there was ever an institution that should be operated on a premise of hope, it's a school. An optimistic school is new every morning. Samuel Adams was known for saying, "What a glorious morning this is." That's what an optimistic school says to students—every morning. It's a place teachers and kids want to be.

What's an optimistic school like? The best explanation I've ever seen was contained in a letter to the editor from the parent of a sixth-grader in Minneapolis:

> *Recently, I was dropping my daughter off at school and she said, "I have never had a bad day at Kenny." After six years of elementary school, I can think of no finer tribute.*

That's an optimistic school. I've never been to Kenny Community School. But I'd like to. Wouldn't you?

Optimism is a choice. All attitudes are. Pessimism is a downer. It's a black hole from which nothing good ever comes. So why choose it?

Optimism can give you an advantage and is a lot more fun. It's free. It's available to everyone. Optimists are the answers to their own prayers. So why not apply the power of optimism to your school?

Best of all, optimism works. It's not just a pie-in-the-sky, feel-good way of living. It's a practical recipe for success in the real world. No business leader, no military leader, no school leader, no leader of any kind can get to the top and stay there without it. So, be optimistic or else!

P's and Q's

Success is the sum of the details.

—Harry S. Firestone
tire manufacturer

Men trip not on mountains, they stumble on stones.

—Hindustani proverb

The story goes that in old English pubs, many revelers preferred to run up a tab. Lacking any more sophisticated method, barkeeps recorded, on a chalkboard or simply on the wall, the number of pints (p's) and quarts (q's) consumed. Obviously, it was prudent for both servers and consumers to monitor the tally closely. Hence, the popular admonition, "mind your p's and q's" became a metaphor for paying attention to details.

Obviously, schools aren't pubs; but it's still good advice today. We've all heard the saying, "the devil is in the detail." As things turn out, it's really true.

Without question, the flat-out, single best way to ensure success, avoid costly mistakes, and "cover your rear" is to attend to details. Little things actually do make a difference. Done right, it's the little things that have the most immediate and long-lasting impact.

Good leaders, in both business and education, recognize the critical significance of paying attention to nuts and bolts and "getting all their ducks in a row." That's why the best principals and supervisors are never too busy to concentrate on pesky, but important, details.

Don't be seduced or misled by the volume of popular self-help literature that advises "don't sweat the small stuff." Some small stuff needs to be sweated!

Nit-picking and being methodical are not the same thing. ("To give great attention to details is the mark of the genius—to putter with trifles is not."—Charles B. Rogers) It's your job to know the difference.

Don't be afraid to take little steps or to put carefully in place the small building blocks necessary to construct grand schemes. There are no shortcuts. You just can't skip essential details.

Successful schools don't explode on the scene overnight as the result of quantum leaps or major breakthroughs in performance. Success usually results from doing lots of little things right. It's the accumulation of numerous small acts (details) that puts winning schools over the top.

Of course, there's no end of details to attend to. But some are obviously more important than others. Below are 15 examples of must-do details that may seem small but can make a big difference in your school:

1. *Give reasons for your actions—not just policy references.* It takes extra time and effort, but it's a necessary detail. Effective school leaders don't settle for hiding behind school rules or the school board policy manual. People want a real explanation, not a bureaucratic runaround. Give it to them.

2. *Answer your own phone.* When most people call your school or office, they don't expect to reach a real human being—let alone talk directly to the administrator they're calling. That's why the best school leaders don't let a phone ring without answering it. You shouldn't either.

When I call the district office of the sprawling Minneapolis (Minnesota) Public Schools and the superintendent picks up on the second ring, it makes a huge positive impression. That's the kind of image you want your school to have.

Answering your own phone shows you take calls seriously, that callers are important to your school, and that you refuse to hide behind a phalanx of intermediaries. It's such a little thing. Or is it?

3. *Call people by name.* There is power in people's names. It is easy for students, and even staff members, to feel powerless and anonymous in the bureaucracy of a large school system and for parents and other residents to feel unrecognized and unimportant.

Fortunately, calling people by name helps dispel feelings of invisibility and irrelevance. It's just a small detail. But it works.

4. *Send handwritten notes.* It doesn't take much time to jot off a quick note of appreciation, encouragement, or congratulations to a student, teacher, secretary, crossing guard, or volunteer, but it's an act that can have a long-lasting impact.

Handwritten notes are personal and powerful. What's said is less important than the fact you wrote it. A simple "Thanks for being a real pro," "I'm in your corner," "Great presentation," or "We couldn't have done it without you" is all it takes.

Of course, the most welcome note is the one the recipient never expected to receive. Writing a handwritten message takes only a few seconds, but it can generate timeless good will.

5. *Be on time.* Being late for meetings, appointments, and school events may be fashionable, but it is also rude, thoughtless, selfish, and disrespectful of others' time. You can do better.

They don't have a Hallmark Card for promptness yet, but they should have. Being on time, every time can earn you a reputation for being responsible, accountable, and considerate.

Best of all, promptness is infectious. It can become part of the school culture. Just think, if everyone in the organization were always on time, productivity would go off the charts, and you would save so much time you wouldn't have to worry anymore about lengthening the school day or the school year.

It doesn't take any more effort to be punctual. It does, however, take a little discipline and some organizational skills. Supposedly, these are traits common to all good school leaders.

6. *Sign your own correspondence.* Using a stamp or having a secretary or assistant sign your name to routine correspondence is easy and efficient. It's also impersonal and bureaucratic. Is that the impression you want to leave with students, staff, parents, or community members?

Adding the extra touch of a handwritten signature sets you apart. It shows you care enough to personally sign off on what you write. It doesn't take much time. It's just a little detail. But it still matters.

7. *Look people in the eye.* In our culture, eye contact denotes interest and respect. Conversely, averting eye contact signals inattention, lack of concern, or dishonesty. Looking others in the eye is the quickest, surest way to establish rapport and respect. It's easy. It's free. It's almost too big a little detail for school leaders to overlook.

8. *Get the "backup habit."* Modern technology is wonderful, but it can turn on you. Think of all the valuable records, data, and information you have stored on school computers. What happens if a virus strikes or if your computer crashes and all the vital stuff is lost? Yikes! If you can't afford to lose it, back it up every time. It's a detail worth sweating over.

9. *Pay attention to punctuation, spelling, and grammar.* Never let written communications leave your office filled with errors or typos. Nothing

sabotages an educator's credibility faster than sending out written materials laced with mistakes.

For example, when a school district where I used to work sent out notices under the lead, "____PUBIC SCHOOLS," it wasn't just an embarrassment. It destroyed the serious tone and distracted from an important message. The error was the first thing readers noticed and the only thing they remembered from the communication. It wouldn't have happened if someone had been paying attention to details.

Worse yet, I've seen important documents come out of a superintendent's office containing spelling and grammatical errors that wouldn't be acceptable in most fourth-grade classes. It's inexcusable, but not unavoidable. If there is ever a place for a policy of zero tolerance for errors, this is it.

10. *Respond promptly.* Returning phone calls and answering e-mail messages in a timely manner are not high priorities for many principals and superintendents. But they should be.

Getting back to people is another mark of courtesy and professionalism that separates superior school leaders from wannabes and also-rans. It seems like a minor issue, but people notice the difference.

11. *Turn off the lights.* Energy cost savings can begin with a flip of the switch. When it's the principal or superintendent who does the flipping, it sends a message that can permeate the entire organization. Economical conservation isn't accomplished through lip service or fancy slogans. It takes lots of little actions—starting at the top. That's where you are.

12. *Remember manners.* If you think good manners are a thing of the past, you're missing a good bet. Manners still matter. "Please" and "Thank you" remain the currency of all smooth-running organizations.

There's a reason that many businesses and MBA-training institutions are now offering courses in good manners and that more and more communities are introducing "Cotillion" programs to teach teens and preteens acceptable social skills. What do these groups know that you don't?

Manners are just one of the details of daily living, but they are another way to model respect for people at all levels. If educators don't demonstrate respect for others, who will?

13. *Meet people halfway.* Don't always make people come to you. Unless you're the Pope, people shouldn't always have to request an audience to get to see you. There's no law that you can't go to them.

There's a message in meeting students, teachers, and parents halfway—or better yet, on their turf. It's a little touch of class that signals you consider them important and value your contacts with them. That's why business gurus advocate MWWA (Management While Walking Around) not MWSA (Management While Sitting Around).

14. *Take a little extra time.* It doesn't take much additional time to do things right the first time. That's why effective school leaders proofread reports one more time, double-check data, and repeat instructions. Little time investments often yield big dividends.

15. *Smile more.* Smiling doesn't require any more exertion of facial muscles than frowning, but it can transform your office or school. If every principal and superintendent in the country would smile more every day, teachers would work harder and happier, and kids would learn more and have more fun. Who knows? We might even achieve world peace.

Obviously, details aren't just nuisances. They are the pieces that make up the puzzle. Leadership isn't only big-picture stuff. It's also seeing to it that the finer points are taken care of. Anyone can have a dream. But it will never become reality until someone works out the details.

If you are not a detail person, get someone on board who is. Every administrative team needs at least one "concrete-sequential" member who is compulsive about focusing on the details, the nuances, and the fine-tuning of leadership.

It also pays to keep lists (use 'em, don't lose 'em) and to allow your calendar, daily planner, and electronic organizer help you keep track of all the endless details. Do whatever it takes to ensure that all the small stuff is covered. It's the only way you can make it as a modern principal or superintendent.

In fact, nailing down all important details preordains success! Yes, you read it right. Once you've done all the necessary minutia, success is virtually guaranteed and almost anticlimactic.

The best leaders in the world agree with Arthur Conan Doyle's observation: "It has long been an axiom of mine that the little things are infinitely the most important." If it's good enough for Sherlock Holmes, it should be good enough for you.

"Mind your P's and Q's" isn't just good advice. It's one of the first laws of longevity for school leaders today. So if you want to succeed and survive in your school, just obey the law.

Q Quid Pro Quo

All politics is local.

—Thomas "Tip" O'Neill
former congressman

This is quite a game, politics. There are no permanent enemies, and no permanent friends, only permanent interests.

—Henry Clay
American politician

The Latin phrase "quid pro quo" means an equal exchange—giving something to get something. What does that have to do with school leadership? Just about everything. It's all about politics.

Educators like to view themselves as professional, diplomatic, and statesmanlike. And they are. But they are also political. They can't help themselves.

Despite what you may wish, you have a political job and you are directly and heavily involved in politics almost every minute of every day. It's not a bad thing.

Every school leader, like every chief executive officer, manager, supervisor, or foreman in business, has a political job. Business leaders recognize, accept, and use this fact to their advantage. School leaders tend to ignore, downplay, or deny it. That's a mistake.

Too many principals and superintendents think of politics as something unsavory. This is a common misconception resulting from the activities of certain highly publicized "dirty politicians" who give all politics a bad name. In reality, politics is neutral. It's a fact of life in all human organizations, including your school.

Politics isn't necessarily the devious practice of duplicity and double-dealing that many people make it out to be. It's just another way leaders get things done.

Ken Blanchard, of "one-minute manager" fame, says that "the key to successful leadership today is influence, not authority." The way leaders influence others is through politics. That's why another acclaimed business writer, Patricia Buhler, adds, "Politics is simply knowing how to deal with people." It's mostly a matter of matching preparation with opportunity to get people to do what you want or need them to do.

The best definition of all may come from the popular television series *Judging Amy.* In one episode, a senior judge explains to a neophyte judge, Amy, that politics is simply "interlocking mutually beneficial relationships." It all starts with reciprocity. That's where quid pro quo comes in.

Reciprocity is the core of most organizational interaction. It's not just in contract negotiations that parties give something for something. It's in every aspect of everyday relationships. It's the way we do business with each other.

People are constantly exchanging favors and trading off concessions. "You scratch my back and I'll scratch yours" isn't just a cute saying. It's the way the world works—even in the cloistered halls of your school.

Effective leaders in every field are never too proud to make deals or too afraid to horse trade. They make the most of reciprocity. You should, too.

Quid pro quo is the currency of organizational leadership—including educational leadership. It works with kids. It works with teachers. It works with unions. It works with the district office. It works. Period.

The trick is to make it work for you. To help make this happen, following are 30 of the best insider tips anyone ever got on handling politics, especially on the art of quid pro quo:

1. Keep a "People File" on all the important people you meet, in and out of the profession. You never know when information on their background, family status, passions, achievements, and interests will come in handy.

2. Honor your commitments. Keep your side of the bargain—every time!

3. Make one new ally every month.

4. Understand the organization. Who has the power? Why? How did they get it? And how do they use it? It usually pays to keep your head down for the first three months on a new job until you learn who the players are, what the rules are, and who your enemies are.

5. Never promise what you can't deliver.

6. Don't give away what's not yours to give.

7. Never underestimate the other guy (especially an opponent). Don't assume anything about anyone. ("If you underestimate an opponent you may get kicked on your butt. If you overestimate an opponent you may be pleasantly surprised."—Jeffrey J. Fox)

8. Be loyal. If you can't, move on.

9. Develop alliances at all levels.

10. Acknowledge any Achilles' heels up front. Reveal bad news or faults before others discover them and infer you have been hiding something.

11. Learn how to schmooze. It's a survival skill for school leaders.

12. Don't hide information from your superiors. No boss likes surprises.

13. Find out how your bosses prefer to receive information. Give them what they need to know in the form they want it.

14. Accept, adapt to, and fit in with the overall style of your superiors. A prime example of "fitting in" is a student I know who cut his long hair before heading off to a conservative Midwest college, saying, "You have to look like them to change them."

15. Give your bosses honest feedback. Otherwise you are useless to them.

16. If at all possible, say "Yes" to whatever the boss requests.

17. Don't count on "kissing up" for your survival. Being a buddy of the boss is no substitute for competence.

18. The best political move is always to make the boss(es) look good. Don't let your boss make a mistake if you can possibly help it. And tell your staff not to let you make any either.

19. Invite your enemies into your inner circle. That way, you know what they are doing. ("I'd rather have you inside the tent pissing out than outside pissing in."—Lyndon B. Johnson)

20. Don't be for sale. Don't compromise your values, principles, or beliefs for perks or personal gain. Some cynics believe that everyone has a price. ("A honest politician is one [who] when he is bought will stay bought."—Simon Cameron) Prove them wrong.

21. Remember that no victory (or defeat) is final. Don't gloat over other people's bad news. Always allow opponents to save face.

22. Make it a code of conduct within your staff to "cover each others' backs."

23. Try not to burn bridges or sever any relationships permanently. ("Never cut what you can untie."—Joseph Joubert)

24. Make friends with the school gossip. That way you will get to hear all the latest inside scoop, while avoiding being the object of rumor or gossip yourself.

25. Use the persuasive power of touch. When you need to get someone to do something, try touching the person softly on the arm as you ask. Most people respond more positively to appropriate touch.

26. Don't make an enemy by mistake. You don't need carelessness, misjudgment, or insensitivity to make enemies for you. Circumstances will do enough of that without any help.

27. Try to stay out of petty internal politics. You can't build a career on minor squabbles or trivial triumphs.

28. Don't become paranoid about politics. Not all opposition is political. Sometimes people just honestly disagree with you.

29. Be wary of giving advice. Some people aren't really looking for counsel. They're looking for accomplices.

30. Don't blame all your defeats on politics. Only poor losers do that.

Politics is everywhere. As a leader's leader, you can't deny it, ignore it, or hide from it. The only question is whether you handle it well or poorly. If you get really good at it, people won't even realize what you are doing.

Politics is simultaneously easier than you may think and more difficult than you may imagine. It's not as easy as just picking the right side. ("Leadership has a harder job to do than just choosing sides. It must bring sides together."—Jesse Jackson)

If you expect to achieve your goals, you must be willing to be political. You have to understand politics and work hard at it every day.

After all, quid pro quo means something for something. Not something for nothing. All good leaders know that. Now, you do, too.

R Removing Obstacles

So much of what we call management consists in making it difficult for people to work.

—Peter Drucker
father of modern management

My job is removing obstacles and challenging people's imagination.

—Leon Royer, project manager
3M Corporation

There must be hundreds of definitions for leadership. You probably have a favorite of your own. For me, the hands-down best definition is simply, "Removing obstacles."

Harvey Mackay, envelope industry mogul and award-winning motivational speaker, maintains that 80 percent of all obstacles to success come from within the organization. He's talking about businesses, but he could easily be referring to schools.

Many schools create roadblocks that prevent them from fulfilling their vision. When that happens, it's the leader's fault. If it happens in your school, that's you.

How you lead either builds barriers and sets traps (gotchas) or knocks down hurdles and makes it easier for everyone to do better what they do best.

You don't need this book to tell you that removing obstacles is the leadership style of choice for all successful principals and superintendents. You already know that.

The real questions are the following: Do you act on that knowledge every day? What have you done lately to make it easier for teachers to teach and students to learn?

If you really want to get better at leading your school, start ripping down barriers, eliminating bottlenecks, hacking away at impediments, removing shackles, sweeping hazards out of the way, running interference, creating safety nets, and giving all the people in your school the protection they need to get their job done. Remove all fear so that no one is afraid to do his or her best and all employees can show what they can do.

The best way to start is to look at the school through the eyes of the students and staff members and work backward from what they need. It can be as easy as asking teachers to list their top five roadblocks or conducting a quarterly student survey asking, "What can the administration do to make school easier and better for you?"

Once obstacles are pinpointed, put them on your "To Do" list, but don't stop there. Anyone can keep a list of things to do. But great leaders also have a "Stop Doing" list that identifies self-defeating behaviors, practices, and procedures that should be abandoned.

Of course, discovering and labeling obstacles is easy. Doing something about them is more difficult. It takes awareness, initiative, risk taking, and a modicum of old-fashioned courage. You can't do it sitting behind a desk, and you will have to get your hands dirty. Not all administrators have the will for it. But the best ones do.

So when you are ready to get started or get better, the 16 sample action steps that follow have been tried in successful schools and businesses across the country. Take your pick. They all work. Some of them may just be what you are looking for.

1. *Reduce bureaucracy.* (Where have you heard that before?) Thin the layers of administration. Blur distinctions between administration, discipline, and counseling. Stress interdepartmental activities. Streamline record keeping. Cut out duplication. Limit regulations, policies, procedures, processes, and red tape. Don't make new rules that punish everyone for the transgressions of a few. Reduce actions that require signoffs or approvals. And cut down on meetings.

Anything you do to remove bureaucratic barriers helps. If you don't keep at them, they will keep popping up and multiplying like weeds. Eventually, they can choke the life out of the school. Without vigilance, the bureaucratic structure can become all there is of the organization.

If you want to be an effective leader, eliminate bureaucracy in your school. If you want to be a bureaucratic, get a job at the Pentagon.

2. *Remove barriers between you and students.* Don't make students always go through an assistant, or even your secretary, to get to you; and don't be a stranger to their turf.

The most damning criticism of a school leader I ever heard came from a high school student who told me she didn't know who her principal was, what her principal's name was, or what her principal looked like.

I may be old-fashioned, but I'm pretty sure that if people don't know who you are, you aren't leading them anywhere. Students (and staff) need a visible leader, not a phantom figurehead.

3. *Model "calendar integrity."* Waiting is wasted time and wasted time is a roadblock you create for yourself. Stick to your schedule. Be prompt for meetings. Don't blow off appointments, and don't keep people waiting. Make being punctual the way you do business in your school.

4. *Give your teachers some "fire power."* Allow them to fire department heads or team leaders who aren't doing their job or fail to provide proper leadership.

Better yet, allow them to fire certain customers (parents). When unreasonable parents unduly harass teachers or demand an inordinate amount of teacher time, it's your responsibility to intervene and provide a buffer. Require that parents who are out of line deal only with you, rather than directly with your staff. Now that's removing an obstacle!

5. *Limit the number of goals.* Business writer Jim Collins suggests that it's better for a leader to have one BHAG (pronounced bee-hag)—Big Hairy Audacious Goal—than a plethora of smaller ones. Most management experts agree.

Having too many goals is as bad as having none. Some schools become immobilized by the sheer number of goals they set for themselves.

When an organization pursues an unmanageable array of objectives, it loses credibility and staff members become overwhelmed, skeptical, and cynical; sometimes they just give up. When teachers and other employees don't know where to start, they often don't.

I recently witnessed a classic example of goal-overkill when a close family member left his power position with a major corporation, largely because of the confusing multiplicity of goals that constantly rained down from corporate headquarters. There was no time to assimilate, let alone implement, one goal before several more descended from on high. Chasing too many goals doesn't work in corporate America, and it won't work in your school either.

Adopting an excessive number of goals creates an obstacle. It isn't planning. It's wishful thinking, and it's a waste of time.

6. *Shred paperwork.* Cut down on the number of reports, the number of copies, the frequency of reports, and the number of recipients.

According to Kelly Spaulding of the Quill Corporation, "Research shows that 45 new sheets of paper are generated each day for every office worker in America—about 1.5 trillion sheets of paper a year." I wouldn't be surprised if teachers generate even more.

Paperwork is an obstacle in most schools. If principals and superintendents don't lead the fight against needless paper mania, who will? Anything you can do to lighten the paper load in your school will free up time for real work with real kids. That's what leaders do.

7. *Set realistic standards.* It's not always heresy to consider lowering your standards. Unreasonably high standards can become an albatross if they discourage people from even trying.

If perfection is your standard, it's not going to happen. Often, perfection is just another name for nit-picking. Lower your standards where appropriate and you just might accomplish more.

8. *Do your own dirty work.* ("Generals dig their own foxholes."— James Caville). When the leader in any organization becomes the center of attention, something more important is being neglected. If people have to spend a lot of time catering to your wishes and whims, you are not only a distraction—you are an obstacle. Take care of your own needs, so others can take care of businesses.

9. *Become a prospector.* The biggest, single obstacle facing most schools today is lack of adequate funding. More than ever, school leaders have to find, raise, or attract extra resources for their school.

Do what the most successful resource brokers and fund finders do: Become visible; go where the money is; tell your story; have a wish list; maximize fees, fines, and fundraisers; go after gifts, grants, and endowments; consider selling advertising; open a school store; tap into booster clubs, alumni associations and educational foundations; and partner with local businesses.

To make it all easier, take a tip from professional fundraisers—always ask for more than you expect to get. Potential donors won't be shocked or scared off. They're usually flattered.

10. *Hire a "free agent."* In business, free agent employees are soloists who hop from project to project, troubleshooting and using their talents wherever they are needed most. They're like the utility player in baseball who can play all the positions.

You need someone like that on your staff—someone who can teach (several subjects), coach, counsel, chair a committee, head-up a fundraising drive, organize the parent-teacher organization, lobby the school board, fill in for the principal, and even drive the school bus if necessary.

Too much specialization can obstruct progress. That's why every school needs at least one versatile generalist. If you don't have a free agent on your staff, make it a hiring priority for the immediate future.

11. *Have a Rule 240.* In airline lingo, Rule 240 refers to what an airline will do in the event of a delay or cancellation. Schools need similar rules spelling out what they will do when they screw up, leave some child behind, or can't deliver. Shortcomings aren't obstacles if you have the plan and the commitment to make things right.

12. *Don't be easy on "clockroaches."* Steve Kraemer, entrepreneur and co-owner of Two Steves Painting in Dayton, Ohio, coined the term, clockroaches, to describe those employees who are as useless as cockroaches but still get paid on your time clock anyway.

These are employees you have to chase down, ask to do something, argue with about doing it, and then check on later to see that it got done. Every school has at least one. It may be a teacher. Or a custodian. Sometimes, heaven forbid, it's the principal.

Clockroaches are real obstacles. They get in the way, slow things down, stack things up, and hold others back. If you can't get rid of your clockroaches, at least place or position them where they will do the least harm.

13. *Focus on the "little picture," too.* Of course, it's important that everyone in the school understands the "big picture" (where the organization is going). But it's equally important that all parties also understand the "little picture" (their role—how their piece of the puzzle fits in). This is especially true of nonteaching personnel, such as clerks, cooks, custodians, security workers, and bus drivers.

When people don't see how their job contributes to fulfilling the vision of the organization, they often feel disconnected, unmotivated, and irrelevant. That's an obstacle no school leader needs.

14. *Avoid micromanagement.* Managerial meddling is obstructive. Don't do it. It makes you part of the problem.

Instead of spending time looking over people's shoulders or breathing down their necks (second guessing, "snoopervising," tinkering, fixing, and correcting), use your time to find ways to unleash their talents. That's the difference between maintenance management and creative leadership.

15. *Make efficiency a priority.* Efficiency is a big deal in businesses. Why not in schools?

Efficiency is simply getting things done quickly, easily, cheaply, and accurately. It means cleaning up and streamlining operating systems to eliminate wasted time, wasted effort, and wasted resources. Who wouldn't want to do that? Obviously, this is one thing that school leaders can learn from business leaders.

A classic example is the Hertz Corporation, which got to be Number 1 because of its phenomenally efficient four-step car checkout system: (1) Leave plane. (2) Ride bus directly to car. (3) Get in prestarted car. (4) Drive away. That's efficiency!

If you can similarly break down and simplify your school's operations (e.g., registration and enrollment, changing classes, inventorying textbooks, grade reporting, or processing teacher applications), you will go a long way in removing obstacles.

Some schools have gone so far as to adopt the Six Sigma system, a rigorous quality improvement program that many businesses use to reduce defects (faulty outcomes) drastically. You may want to check it out.

With or without any special programs, you can maximize efficiency in your school. It's another way to make the school better without spending more money.

16. *Never rest on your laurels.* Past successes can be an obstacle to future successes if you stop there and continue to coast on yesterday's triumphs. Laurels are to build on, not rest on. Success needs a fresh coat of paint every day.

Removing obstacles, such as those listed here, is the core of day-to-day school leadership. Unfortunately, as mentioned earlier, the school—your school—often creates many of its own obstacles. The famous cartoon figure Pogo said it first: "We have met the enemy and it is us." But Pulitzer-nominated journalist Noah benShea may have said it best: "Most of us are the load we are carrying."

That's the reason the Hippocratic Oath forbids physicians from doing anything that might make the patient worse. All educators should take a similar oath. The idea is to remove barriers, not erect them.

If avoiding, removing, or overcoming obstacles sounds like a lot of hard work, it is. It's not glamorous. It's not always exciting. It's grunt work. But do it anyway. It's your job. It's what leaders do.

The reality in your school is that if you are not eliminating obstacles every day, you are not leading. Anything less makes you the obstacle.

S Straight Talk

Communication always sucks.

—Tom Peters
management gadfly

More yacking doesn't guarantee understanding.

—Bill Jensen
author of *Simplicity*

Precision of speech is important, more important than ever before, in an era of hair-trigger balances, where a false or misunderstood word may create as much a disaster as a sudden thoughtless act.

—James Thurber
humorist

Great leaders—including great school leaders—use a secret weapon that many of their counterparts in similar positions ignore or don't know about. It's called straight talk . . . plain English . . . shirtsleeve communication.

It's a simple, but amazingly powerful, tool that gives successful leaders an edge and allows them to win the war of words every time. And words are what much of leadership is all about.

Some people think that leaders should use technical terms, flowery speech, fancy language, or ethereal oratory in order to sound like a leader. Actually, the exact opposite is true. The only thing that leaders really need to do is be clear. That requires no-nonsense, no frills straight talk—and not much else.

Leadership is communication. It's what leaders do for a living. While the average person may speak or write up to 18,000 words each day, that's just a warm-up for most leaders. Principals and superintendents know this better than anybody.

When leaders, in any field, fail to communicate fully, accurately, and understandably—misinformation, misinterpretation, misunderstandings, and mixed messages run rampant. The result is costly confusion. That's not leadership; it's chaos (better known as anti-leadership).

That's why successful managers, supervisors, and administrators, in both the public and private sectors, latch on to straight talk to get the right message across to the right people at the right time, every time.

Unfortunately, many school officials seem unaware of the superior firepower of plain speech or are afraid to use it, because it might make them sound "unprofessional." Educators are infamous for sending out messages that miss the point.

This is alarming in an enterprise designed to help people understand unfamiliar subjects. But it happens every day. It could be happening in your school as you read this. Are you sure it isn't?

If you think I'm exaggerating the problem, consider the following observation on edu-leaders from a friendly source:

What People Dislike

Q. What do people dislike about communicating with politicians?
A. Their propensity for vague answers, noncommittal responses, spin doctoring, and dodging issues.

Q. What do people dislike about communicating with physicians?
A. Their habit of using unfamiliar words, talking down to people, and not listening.

Q. What do people dislike about communicating with ministers?
A. Their long-winded discourse, moralizing judgments, and obscure references.

Q. What do people dislike about communicating with techies?
A. Their retreat into a language all their own and lack of effort to demystify their communication.

Q. What do people dislike about communicating with educators?
A. ALL OF THE ABOVE!

This comparison may be overly harsh. But it's true enough to make many of us squirm.

In any school environment, communication is the life's blood of the organization. Yet all school leaders fail to be understood sometimes. A few even make a habit of it. You probably know some of them.

If you would like to become a sharper, more effective school leader overnight, just dust off your straight talk. It works every time, and it doesn't cost a thing.

A good place to start is becoming aware of the most common pitfalls that most frequently ensnare educators and snarl their communications. That's why, in *How to Say the Right Thing Everytime*, I pinpointed the 20 most serious communications errors made by school leaders. An abridged version bears repeating here:

THE TOP TWENTY REASONS
EDUCATORS FAIL TO COMMUNICATE

(No priority ranking intended or implied.)

1. *Overuse of jargon.* "Educationese" is a specialized language comprising technical educational terms. Some educators have been known to hide behind it. The best leaders, however, use it sparingly; when school officials use an insider language, they leave everyone else out.

2. *Walking on eggs.* School personnel are notorious for soft-pedaling issues, skirting unpleasant topics, and pussyfooting around sensitive subjects to avoid hurting someone's feelings, making anyone mad, or rocking the boat too much. It seldom works. And often makes things worse.

3. *Bending over backward to be politically correct.* Some educators have neutered their language so much to avoid offending anyone that important meanings get distorted, lost, or go unsaid altogether. Real problems never get solved by muted dialogue or conversations never held.

4. *Too much formality.* When principals or superintendents adopt a professorial tone and talk like a textbook, listeners shut down. But when they use ordinary, everyday language, they capture and keep their listeners' attention.

5. *Overgeneralization.* All educators know the fallacy (and danger) of labeling and stereotyping. Nevertheless, some persist in doing it. School personnel cannot affect individuals by relying on generalities.

6. *Sermonizing.* There's a difference between teaching and preaching. Some school leaders cross the line. Most people tune out pontification. There's a reason so many people fall asleep in church.

7. *Obfuscation.* Too many school administrators beat around the bush—like a former colleague who prided himself on his ability to "vague things up." Someone should have told him that vagueness isn't on the list of accepted leadership goals. Obfuscators spread a fog in which most listeners get lost.

8. *Being dogmatic.* Nobody likes to listen to a know-it-all. So they don't. Even if it's the principal or superintendent. Real leaders help people discover their own truths and draw their own conclusions, rather than shoving preconceived notions down their throats.

9. *Patronizing.* Too many people feel that educational leaders are condescending. It's hard to look up to a leader who talks down to you.

10. *Making empty threats.* An empty threat is a promise that can't be kept. We've all seen administrators make them and break them. Weak teachers threaten what they can't deliver. So do weak leaders. It's always a bad idea.

11. *Whining.* Educators, at all levels, whine a lot (not entirely without just cause). Unfortunately, it's never effective, only annoying. There are better ways to build a case for improvement.

12. *Grammatical and spelling errors.* School leaders lose credibility when they make simple mechanical errors in communication. It happened to a superintendent I knew who routinely made usage mistakes such as, "I can't *phantom* why it happened."

His gaffes were part of his charm, but they also distracted from his message and bothered many listeners. A key role of any administrative team should be to keep their leader from making such costly miscues.

13. *Lying and denying.* School officials typically don't do a great deal of lying, but they do a lot of denying. Denial of the obvious makes any leader look like a liar, a fool, or both. Take your pick. You lose either way. Effective leaders own up to shortcomings or judgmental errors (if you transgress, confess) and face up to unpleasant truths. It's the only way to build believability and trust.

14. *Overload.* Too much information is as bad as too little information. Some school leaders negate their message by saying too much.

15. *Overuse of "slanguage."* A little slang can spice up your message. But more isn't better. Using too much only makes you appear juvenile and less professional. I've seen administrators overdo it. So have you. It's not a pretty sight.

16. *Showing off.* Some principals and superintendents think it's leaderlike to bowl people over with their multisyllabic vocabulary. They're wrong. Good leaders prefer to use recognizable words in recognizable ways. That way, they are actually understood.

17. *Being cute.* We've all known administrators who try to come across as cute and fall short. Cute is a tiny target. And there is nothing more lame or pathetic than someone who shoots for cute—and misses. It's a surefire way to stop being taken seriously.

18. *Using profanity.* School personnel who use profanity for its shock value are taking a risk. In print (e.g., #?@%!), it's sometimes palatable, but when listeners hear it spoken out loud by a respected school leader, it often embarrasses and offends the audience.

19. *Overfamiliarization.* Some administrators feign intimacy in an attempt to make their communication seem more personal. It backfires more often than it works.

Trying to appear chummier than you really are in assuming a closeness that doesn't exist is a lie. And everyone knows it and resents it.

20. *Sexual innuendos.* What can I say? This is absolutely the stupidest communication blunder any school official can make. Yet some persist in using sexual references to gain attention. Sensible leaders never go out on that limb, because that's where the sap is.

From this entire list of common communication errors, what drives laymen most crazy is the overuse of jargon and euphemisms. Hiding behind semi- or pseudo-scientific jargon (e.g., "multisensory approach," "criterion-referenced tests," or "affective domain") is a sign of insecurity, cowardice, or arrogance. It is insulting and intimidating to many people.

Every audience deserves the truth in understandable terms, not mumbo jumbo. As head of the school, it is your responsibility to translate unwieldy educationese into layman's language. A good place to start is by making school finance terminology understandable to civilians.

Like jargon, euphemisms only muddle the message. Some edu-leaders use them because they want to be kind. Who wants to deliver bad news? Many would rather be a nice guy—even if it means protecting people who aren't doing the job. But softening the blow beyond recognition isn't kindness, it's cowardice, and it's dishonest.

Strong leaders aren't afraid to be honest—even if it is initially painful and unpleasant. Problems don't get solved until people are willing to discuss them openly and frankly. It's fun to be Mr. Nice Guy, but it's more important to be a real leader doing real communication.

Plain speech isn't always pretty, but it clears the air and gets the message across. It communicates. That's what leaders are paid to do. The all-time best advice is to use euphemisms very sparingly. Try the truth instead. It's hard to improve on honesty.

The remedy for most of the communication ills above is just to "keep it simple." Sound easy? It's not. But straight talk can make you a better leader. Period!

Straight talk makes a difference because it saves time, eliminates confusion, builds trust, and establishes credibility. ("Learn to speak and write in plain English. Long, tedious, flowery, jargon-filled communications are wasteful."—Jeffrey J. Fox) Best of all, straight talk is understood and believed. It is the language for all seasons and all ages.

Straight talk works with kids because they can spot phonies a football field away and have a built-in "bull" detector. Students have no patience with double-talk and appreciate being leveled with. It makes them feel valued and respected.

Straight talk works with parents because you need their support and understanding. Without that, you have no viable school. Parents want to help. But only if they believe and trust you. Being vague and noncommittal won't win them over. Neither will side-stepping hard facts or issues. Nor will dragging out all the big words you know. But plain talk and honest answers will.

Straight talk works with staff members because meaningful, internal dialogue is critical to school success. Every school staff—even yours—needs more honest conversation. Without it, what begs to be said and needs to be heard will go unsaid, unheard, and unattended to.

And straight talk works with the public, because it's what community members want, what they understand, and, in most cases, what they demand. If the public doesn't believe what the school has to say, educational excellence is out of the question, and even mediocrity is a long shot.

All this makes straight talk too good a deal for you or any other school leader to miss out on. And think of this: Speaking and writing plainly, clearly, and with total candor is so rare and unprecedented that it can immediately set you apart. Becoming known as a straight shooter (truth teller) can elevate you to the top of the heap quicker than a balanced budget.

Of course, if straight talk were easy, everyone would do it. Obviously, they don't. Maybe because it takes forethought, practice, and discipline. But it's worth it.

So if you decide you want to become a better straight-talk communicator (and a better school leader at the same time), use the following 21 "must-do" tips to get started on the right track:

1. Say what people need to hear—not just what they want to hear.

2. Tailor communication to specific individuals or groups. To be effective, communication has to be audience-appropriate.

3. Get to the point.

4. Use your own words.

5. Remember that how you say something is as important as what you say.

6. Talk to people, not at them.

7. Limit the number of messages you try to send at one time.

8. Make every word count.

9. Give preference to small, household words.

10. If you must use technical terms, define them in plain language.

11. Use plenty of real-world examples.

12. Always choose the simplest version.

13. If you are not sure it's true, don't act as if it is.

14. Come forward with bad news as promptly as you do with good news.

15. Admit mistakes. Take blame. The sooner, the better.

16. Avoid "cheap shots."

17. Don't repeat rumors and gossip as fact.

18. Beware that half-truths are also half-lies.

19. Give real reasons, not policy references.

20. Lighten up and tighten up. Don't take yourself too seriously and don't drone on and one.

21. If it doesn't feel right, don't say it.

Naturally, it's not just educational leaders who need to rediscover straight talk. Business and political leaders do, too. For example, in their popular political primer, *Buck Up, Suck Up . . . And Come Back When You Foul Up,* James Carville and Paul Bagala offer these simple rules for "great communication":

- Tell a story.
- Be brief. (Sound bites work. After all, John 3:16 and the Golden Rule are nothing but sound bites.)
- Be emotional.
- Be relevant (Answer "so what?").
- Repeat your message relentlessly.

These rules can help politicians and business leaders get their message across. They can help school leaders, too. My favorite guide to straight talk, however, is this simple seven-step Code of Communication:

1. Say only what's true.

2. Say what needs to be said.

3. Say what you mean.

4. Say it to the right people.

5. Say it as soon as possible. (Timeliness is next to Godliness.)

6. Say it as simply as possible.

7. Keep on saying it.

These steps look harmless. But they constitute a high-powered secret weapon you can use to improve your leadership and your school.

Of course, there are lots of good reasons for you to opt for straight talk. But the most important may be because it's your job to get everyone in the organization to see the world as it is, not as they want or wish it to be. This requires frequent reality checks and a lot of old-fashioned, plain English.

That's why straight talk is the language of choice for all successful leaders today. If you are not using it, start now. I can't make it much plainer than that.

T Teflon
Tenacity

Nothing in the world can take the place of persistence. Talent will not; nothing is more common than unsuccessful men with talent. Genius will not; unrewarded genius is almost a proverb. Education will not; the world is full of educated derelicts. Persistence and determination are omnipotent. The slogan "press on" has solved and always will solve the problems of the human race.

—Calvin Coolidge
former U.S. president

Change is good. Change is healthy. It's exciting. It's imperative for survival and crucial to success. It's even inevitable. But wait a minute. Too much change is distracting, disruptive and confusing.

Leadership isn't just about changing things. It's also about staying the course when it counts. Persistence pays off, too. Especially, if you are running a school.

News anchor Dan Rather says, "To win a war, you need (1) fire power, (2) will power, and (3) staying power." Of these three, staying power may be the most important.

Your school isn't a war zone (OK, it is sometimes), but persistence or tenacity still makes a difference. Whether you are in charge of a single school or an entire school system, it takes the persistent pursuit of worthwhile causes, ideas, and goals to produce maximum results.

Good leaders stay at it until they achieve desired outcomes. They see things through. If you don't believe it, you probably won't be around long enough to discover how true it is.

There are always a lot of good reasons to waffle, waver, hesitate, withhold or withdraw support, slack off, back off, back up, back away, back down, or quit altogether. But there are many better reasons to persist on

129

matters that really matter. Also-rans pull up short. Winners persist. Here are a dozen reasons why:

1. Most worthwhile projects—especially big changes—take longer than anticipated. If you don't keep pressing forward, they won't happen.

Even the guru of one-minute-management, Ken Blanchard, acknowledges the need for tenacity: "Empowerment isn't magic. It consists of a few simple rules and a lot of persistence." Success is usually a long march. Only the tenacious ever cross the finish line.

2. It takes time to build relationships and support.

3. It takes time to sell ideas.

4. It takes time to develop talent and expertise.

5. It takes time to learn. ("Champions have to make lots of tries and consequently suffer some failures or the organization won't learn."—Tom Peters and Robert Waterman)

Note: If you are not willing to take the necessary time for Numbers 2 through 5—to build relationships, sell ideas, develop talent, and engage in essential learning—you're not persistent enough to persevere. If you can't pass this tenacity test, let someone else lead.

6. People don't get it the first time. It takes persistent repetition to get through to all stakeholders. Have you noticed how persistent advertisers are? It may be annoying, but it works. Dare to be a pest to get your message across or to get others to understand or do what's necessary.

7. Kanter's Law: "Every undertaking looks like a failure in the middle."—Professor Rosabeth Kanter, Harvard Business School.

According to Dr. Kanter, in every important project, there comes a time when it looks hopeless. This is the point where fainthearted school officials get tired, lose faith, and give up. But this is also the precise point at which the best leaders in the land hunker down and press fiercely forward with renewed effort. Good leaders don't stop short or give up too soon. It's not stubbornness. It's persistence. And it's what it takes to get the job done.

8. Making a decision is the easy part. Making it stick takes time. That's where tenacity comes in.

9. Incremental results pick up steam as they go along. It takes persistence to build momentum.

10. Sticking to your beliefs over time is the only way they can become reality.

11. Persistence shows what you stand for. It's another name for stability and commitment. If you are not consistent and persistent, people don't know which leader is going to show up on any given day. That's not leadership. It's playing guessing games.

12. And the greatest reason of all for being tenacious is simply because most people aren't. A good part of success is a matter of outlasting and wearing down the opposition.

If these arguments aren't enough to persuade you of the power of persistence, persist a little longer. It gets better.

What leaders—school leaders, business leaders, all leaders—need today is "Teflon tenacity"—the ability to stick to it without it sticking to you. Ronald Reagan had it. The media even referred to him as the "Teflon President."

As president, Reagan accomplished some formidable goals (e.g., helping to end the Cold War) largely by refusing to be deterred or detoured by negative distractions or diversions. He didn't allow allegations, accusations, innuendos, investigations, scandals, or vicious rumors to get him off course.

It was as if bad things going on in government had nothing to do with him. Reagan acted as if they didn't matter. His unwavering focus on big goals made other embarrassments seem petty and unimportant.

Criticism didn't stick to Reagan. He sloughed it off. His determination (persistence) acted as a protective shield. (Does the word Teflon come to mind?)

Teflon tenacity worked for Ronald Reagan. It can work for you, too. When the excrement hits the fan, stick to business and less of the nasty stuff will stick to you.

Persistence is a virtue all successful school leaders should have. Actually, all successful school leaders already have it. Tenacity is a precondition for success.

Of course, it's hard to remain focused and driven all the time. Americans are notorious for their short attention spans. Principals and superintendents are not exempt. It's always tempting to lighten up, let up, or let go. Don't.

Even the most disciplined school officials occasionally need a tenacity booster shot. When it happens to you, the insights and advice that follow can pump up your persistence. Give these a try:

1. Persistence requires patience. Be willing to wait. Teachers use "wait time" (allowing time for students to come up and come forward with the right answer) every day in the classroom. There's no school-board policy that says administrators can't apply the same principle.

2. Persistence also requires faith that you will prevail. Maybe not immediately. But some day. Keep the faith. If you need a refresher course, reread section "O," "Optimism or Else."

3. Say "No" to some good opportunities if they will pull you away from your central themes.

4. Don't give up on people or ideas as long as they hold promise of moving the school toward desired goals. Give lots of second chances.

5. Overcome idea-killers (see examples). If your school is like most, it has its share of naysayers. Don't let them distract, divert, or discourage you. Idea-killers will destroy you if you let them. Don't let them.

Don't give in. Don't let up. Don't let the idea-killers whittle you into mediocrity. Think boldly. Execute enthusiastically. Battle the inertia . . .

—Jeffrey J. Fox
How to Become CEO

Examples of Idea-Killers Found in Every School

- There's no money.
- Somebody already did it.
- No one else is doing it.
- The time isn't right.
- The board won't like it.
- The teachers won't like it.
- The parents won't like it.
- The taxpayers won't like it.
- The kids won't like it.
- Let's do a survey.
- Apply for a grant.
- How about a committee?
- It's good in theory, but . . .

Source: Adapted from suggestions by Charles (Chic) Thompson, *What a Great Idea.*

6. Stick to what you understand and know you can do. Don't let flattery, ego, ambition, or false pride define what you undertake or seduce you into straying off course.

7. Don't jump on or get stampeded by all the latest fads. Following the hottest fashions isn't leadership; it's knee-jerk management. Don't just follow trends. Set some of your own.

8. Make being deliberate (methodical) part of your style. It's the first step toward the habit of persistence.

9. Don't manage by poll results. Lead by principle, not by fickle popular opinion. Pollsters are merely reporters and repeaters. They identify what people think at the moment, not necessarily what really is or what can be.

Use polls to develop strategy and guide short-term decision making, but not to set the future course for your school.

10. Align what you think and believe with what you say and do. If you do it every day, you can't go wrong. It's called authenticity. And it's what makes persistence possible.

Of course, no matter what you do, being persistent isn't always easy. And it isn't always fun. But it is always necessary. If it didn't take persistence to succeed, the winners' circle would be a lot more crowded.

If you still harbor a shadow of a doubt about the need for tenacity by school leaders, it may be time for one more lesson from your counterparts in business.

Researcher Jim Collins has studied the difference between good companies that remain just that, and those few good companies that step up a notch to become truly *great* companies. What he found is that great firms shy away from lots of changes, twists, and turns or wrenching restructuring. They tend to be steadfast—persistent.

Collins likens it to the famous essay on "The Hedgehog and the Fox" by Isaiah Berlin. According to Berlin, the fox knows many things. He is clever, scheming, and pursues many ends simultaneously. He is scattered. Conversely, the hedgehog knows one big thing. Hedgehogs are focused, plodding, and determined. Guess who has the edge?

Great businesses are more like hedgehogs than like foxes. So are great schools. Isn't greatness what you want for your school? Persistence can make all the difference.

We've all heard that the first rule for success is to "show up." What we haven't all heard is that the second rule is to "show up again." And the third rule is "keep showing up until you succeed." Good leaders resist, insist, and persist.

If you are not persistently pursuing the school's mission, you are leading only halfheartedly. That's not good enough for your school—or any school. You can't be persistent part time.

If you are not persistent now, it is never too late to work on the trait. If you are already persistent, keep it up.

U U-Turns

If you're going in the wrong direction, God allows U-turns.

—Unknown

Change is inevitable, except from a vending machine.

—Bumper sticker

It's not just the Space Shuttle that has to make midcourse corrections. Organizations do, too. Sooner or later, your school will have to as well. Are you ready?

There is no end of possible causes (e.g., internal and external changes, reversals, setbacks, windfalls, or new opportunities) that can make it necessary for a school to switch course or veer off down new pathways.

You never know when priorities will change; new needs will arise; a referendum will fail; test scores will plummet; a court decision will change the rules; the state will adopt new graduation standards; a more liberal school board will take over; a more conservative school board will take over; parents will challenge your curriculum; new research will cast doubts on some of your programs; the school district will adopt new goals; congress will pass added mandates; or the government will pull the plug on your favorite program; or the worst-case scenario will become reality.

Any or all of these things and more can happen any time to any school—even yours. When they do, it's the leader's responsibility (obligation) to help the organization shift gears and alter its course.

Into the life of every school leader, there comes a time—probably several times—to make a midcourse correction. Persistence in pursuing significant goals is important, but you also need to know that good leaders are never afraid of U-turns.

Of course, it's not easy to turn an organization around. Some writers say it's like trying to "herd cats." Change is scary. It's unfamiliar and unpredictable. There are no certainties or signposts. ("There is no road map for unexplored territory."—Bill Gates)

That's why most people in every organization—not just half the people, but a vast majority, over 90 percent—fear change. If that 90-plus percent includes the leader, change is stifled. An organization can move only as fast as the slowest person in it. If that person is at the top, it doesn't move at all.

Human resistance creates friction within the organization that must be overcome before significant movement is possible. That's why change is a slow process, not an event. It takes time to make a U-turn.

Reversing direction in any school, regardless of size, is a little like turning around an ocean liner. You have to plan ahead, start as soon as possible, and allow plenty of time and space to complete the turn.

Naturally, all major changes come at a cost, but leaders who stick around very long know that the cost of not changing can be much greater.

Resisting a change when it's time has come is an exercise in futility. It's beyond your control. Despite the obstacles, whether it's time for a moderate midcourse correction or a complete 180 degree turnaround, leaders must be ready to act. No organization can make a U-turn until someone steers. In your school, that's you.

In smooth-sailing times, school leaders may be able to manage by momentum. But in times of repositioning, it takes more. That's when true leaders earn their keep. ("When things are at risk, and shifting, and you're at a tipping point—that's when leadership is recognized."—Michael O'Brien, Cincinnati-based business consultant)

When it's time for a U-turn, the staff, the school board and the community expect the principal or superintendent to take the wheel. ("A leader is one who knows the way, goes the way and shows the way."—John C. Maxwell) Anything less and you're not leading, you're just along for the ride.

To steer your school in a new direction, the first thing you have to change is your mind. Managing change requires fast thinking, fast decision making and fast execution.

That's another argument for operating with a compressed bureaucracy (flattened-out hierarchy). When "the times are a-changing," the most nimble organization is most likely to survive and succeed.

Like any good driver, effective school leaders are always prepared to make a quick U-turn on short notice. Constant readiness requires a commitment to lifelong learning, a willingness to question conventional wisdom, and the courage to forget everything you think you know in order to grasp new knowledge. ("The illiterate of the 21st century will not be those who cannot read or write, but those who cannot learn, unlearn, and relearn."—Alvin Toffler)

It also helps to have a ready-made response plan. Great leaders are great believers in Plan B. Contingency plans for quick reaction and damage control can be your best U-turn insurance.

Of course, some principals and superintendents simply refuse to change. They not only persist in riding a dead horse; they insist on being buried with it. Instead of going with the flow, they try to dam it up. They don't do any of the right things. Worse yet, they do all the wrong things. You can do better. For your school's sake, you have to.

When a change in direction is necessary or desirable, you may not know exactly what to do, but you should know exactly what not to do. In case you've forgotten, here are three of the worst responses misguided school leaders make when faced with undertaking a major makeover of their school:

1. *Runaway* (physically or emotionally). The keys to leading any organization through a U-turn (structured change) are presence and visibility.

2. *Deny the obvious.* Some things can't be ignored or covered up. Think Richard Nixon.

3. *Keep doing what you're doing.* According to Tom Demarco, a New York and London–based management consultant, the First Law of Mismanagement is, "If something isn't working, do more of it." This is one law you definitely want to break.

All midcourse corrections are different. There is no definitive driver's manual for making organizational U-turns. But some of the best advice comes from the business world.

Change is just business-as-usual for most CEOs and managers in the private sector. They've "been there and done that" many times. So this is another area where educators can definitely learn from business experts. Harvey Mackay (author, lecturer, CEO) is a good one to start with.

When circumstances dictate that you react, change or reverse course quickly, Mackay offers the following suggestions:

- Keep calm.
- Put things in perspective.
- Don't procrastinate.
- Analyze the situation. (Break into manageable pieces.)
- Put it in words.
- Avoid blaming or shaming.
- Be realistic.

- Get informed help. (That's what mentors are for.)
- Involve everyone who is affected, including yourself as leader. (When people are in the loop, they feel they "own" the change.)
- Give clear directions. Answer all questions.
- Assume nothing. Explain and demonstrate everything.
- Keep a sense of humor.

Another helpful approach that business leaders sometimes use in making U-turns is simply to reframe the question. Turn it around. Ask it in a new way. Try to see the situation from a different point of view.

In his book for business leaders, *Weird Ideas That Work,* Robert Sutton describes the process as Vu Ja De (the opposite of déjà vu). It allows you to experience the familiar as if it were new and to see the situation from a different angle. A fresh perspective can lead to out-of-the-box thinking that can lead to out-of-the-box doing. That's what U-turns are all about.

If you want more on what business leaders think about change, check out the popular parable *Who Moved My Cheese?* by Dr. Spencer Johnson. Although it's a long-running best-seller for business readers, it's not off limits for educators. In it, Spencer shares this insight and advice on dealing with U-turns:

- Change happens.
- Anticipate change.
- Adapt quickly.
- Change.
- Enjoy change.
- Be ready to change again and again.

That pretty much sums up the life of a leader (any leader) today. If you are not living and leading this way in your school, you may already be well on your way to becoming irrelevant.

Likewise, if you think using parables to help an organization is a little far out, you may be missing a good bet.

For example, Charles Bates, a St. Paul author and business advisor, has had considerable success helping large corporations change by using a mix of yoga philosophy, organizational theory, and fairy tales. Bates uses stories to encourage executives to focus on how best to serve those they lead. His book, *Pigs Eat Wolves,* is a good example that has become a must-read classic in many business circles.

Of course, parables and fairy tales may not work with your staff. But the point is that successful business leaders are never too proud to use whatever works to turn their organization around. Creative school leaders (That includes you, doesn't it?) should do the same.

When it's time for your school to switch direction, the important thing is to get started. Even if you don't know exactly where you're going. (You probably won't know at first.) There's no law that says you can't make it up as you go along.

There is no pat formula, but there are some tricks of the trade that can help ease you through any U-turns you have to make, such as the following:

• *Refuse to panic.* Notice this was Harvey MacKay's first suggestion as well. It bears repeating.

• *Don't rush things.* There is value in a quick response. But there is even greater value in the right response. Don't make hasty choices just for speed's sake. When you shoot from the hip, you are more likely to shoot yourself in the foot.

• *Focus on the moment.* If you think too much about the future, you may miss your turn. Concentrate first on the here and now. Author E. J. Ourso calls it letting your imagination "work overtime on the near-at-hand."

• *Signal your turn.* Tell people (everyone involved) the truth about what's going on, where you're going, why you're going, and how you're going to get there.

• *Put your best people to work on making the change.* Go with the best talent, not necessarily with those who have the most prestigious titles.

• *Listen to your intuition.* Gut feelings are most valuable in periods of great uncertainty, few precedents, many choices, limited time, and mounting pressure. God gives you hunches for a reason. Let yours work for you.

• *Ask dumb questions.* They often reveal smart answers.

• *Apply the 4-step "PORT" model* that specialists in "resilience education" use to teach kids how to thrive in adversity: (1) *Participation* (engage in the moment), (2) *Observation* (note your experience), (3) *Reflection* (interpret your experience), and (4) *Transformation* (make necessary changes).

• *Radiate confidence.* If the leader doesn't have it, no one will.

No school can continue in the same path indefinitely. No school should want to. The future always lies in new directions. Face it. Your school will have to reinvent itself—maybe more than once—while you are in charge.

It's not a question of whether your school will make a U-turn. It's a question of how soon, how often, and how well you will execute the turn.

Like many of you, I've seen many U-turns in my career. I've seen schools go from racial segregation to full integration. I've seen secondary schools go from traditional scheduling to a modular-flexible (mod-flex) schedule. And back again.

I've see reading programs go from a phonics approach to a whole language emphasis. And back again. I've seen junior highs become middle schools. And neighborhood K–6 schools transformed into paired K–3, 4–6 schools. I've seen conventional schools change to magnet or charter schools. And low-tech schools become high-tech schools. In each of these transformations, the leader has made all the difference.

With a confident, committed, passionate leader, changes come and go without a hitch. But with a tentative, waffling, unsure, noncommittal leader, it's always a bumpy road. There's no such thing as a halfhearted U-turn.

You've ridden with drivers who swerve into a U-turn taking everyone by surprise, jerking them around, and shaking up everything on board. Other drivers make the same turn smoothly and effortlessly, without disturbing anything very much, so that riders hardly know they've changed direction. It's all in the hands of the driver. When it's your school that's turning, those are your hands.

Changing direction is one responsibility you can't duck or delegate. You're in the driver's seat. The truth is that your school can't make a U-turn until *you* turn.

V Vision and Vocabulary

The very essence of leadership is that you have a vision ... You can't blow an uncertain trumpet.

—Father Theodore Hesburgh

Aim high! It's no harder on your gun to shoot the feathers off an eagle than to shoot the fur off a skunk.

—Troy Moore

Make your plans as fantastic as you like, because 25 years from now, they will seem mediocre. Make your plans 10 times as great as you first planned, and 25 years from now you will wonder why you didn't make them 50 times as great.

—Henry Curtis

Oh, no! Not that vision thing again. Have you ever wondered why books on leadership spend so much time on vision? Have you ever thought to yourself, "Hogwash! This vision stuff doesn't have much to do with the real world I work in every day." If so, you're not paying enough attention.

There is a powerful reason why leadership experts write about visioning. Leadership and vision are inseparable. You can't have one without the other. ("Leadership is the capacity to translate vision into reality."—Warren G. Bennis)

Leading an organization isn't like a game of Blind Man's Bluff where you lurch around blindly, hoping to stumble onto something by chance.

There may be some schools run that way, but you don't want anything to do with them.

That's why I can't let you off the hook on the subject. So suck it up and read on. Here's an abridged version of "Vision for Dummies."

A successful vision is nothing more than simply knowing what you want your school to become. It doesn't have to be anything fancy, elaborate, earthshaking, or even original.

A vision just has to be an uplifting, long-term target that can become a self-fulfilling prophecy. It really is true that whatever you can visualize, you can realize. Envisioning a better organization significantly increases the likelihood of it actually happening.

Most compelling visions begin at the top. All great organizations were first someone's grand vision. In business, the great companies (e.g., Disney, FedEx, Home Depot, etc.) didn't just end up that way. They started out that way—in some leader's mind. It works exactly the same way in schools.

Tom Watson, founder of IBM, describes it best: "IBM was fashioned from the template of my vision . . . at the very beginning, I had a clear picture of what the company would look like when it was finally done. You might say I had a model of what it would look like when the dream—my vision was in place."

A clear and convincing vision can energize people, drive action, and catapult the organization from what it is to what it can be. ("people are unstoppable when they are moved by a common vision."—from a United Technologies corporate brochure.)

Somewhere along the way, a strong, shared vision ceases to be just an idea or a dream, and becomes a driving force.

Some administrators think that all this talk about a vision is ethereal woolgathering or pie-in-the-sky wishful thinking. Far from it. There's nothing more down-to-earth and pragmatic than knowing where you're going.

Having a positive image for a better school can

- Shape plans, direct energy, and focus resources.
- Create probabilities out of possibilities.
- Reveal opportunities others miss.
- Give you a standard to measure the present against.
- Tell you the right thing to do.
- Keep your school new every day.

It doesn't get much more practical than that.

A vision isn't just a bunch of words. But the words you use are important. How you talk about it makes a huge difference. What you say and how you say it can go a long way in determining whether or not the vision ever comes true.

Listen to how successful leaders talk about their dreams for their organization. Winners use the language of certainty. They avoid tentative talk—no *ifs*, *maybes*, or *hopefullys*. They don't talk as if their vision might come true. They speak as if it's a sure thing.

If you want to give your vision a running start, talk about it in terms of confidence and commitment. Stress unifying and team-building terms such as *we*, *us*, and *together*. Avoid hollow generalities and cutesy labels. And use lots of power words and phrases (see examples).

Power Words

Achieve	Faith	Optimum	Success
Accomplish	Fresh Start	Optional	Support
Advantage	Fulfillment	Passion	Surpass
Believe	Future	Pay-off	Talent
Best	Goals	Performance	Tools
Better	Growth	Possible	Triumph
Celebrate	Health	Potential	Unique
Challenge	Help	Pride	Unusual
Change	Inspire	Quest	Values
Choice	Journey	Questioning	Victory
Confidence	Joy	Reach	Vision
Commitment	Knowledge	Reinvent	Winning
Decision	Learning	Resiliency	World Class
Desired	Mastery	Skills	Xtra
Dream	Maximum	Special	Young
Encourage	Meaningful	Standards	Zenith
Exceed	Measurable	Strategy	
Expectations	New	Strengths	
Extraordinary	Noteworthy	Stretch	

Champions in all fields use positive self-affirmations to pump themselves up to achieve peak performance and set new records. Organizations can do the same thing. If you convince yourself and others that the dream can happen, don't be surprised when it does.

Make the vocabulary of your vision a part of everyday conversation in your school. Cheerlead. The more you talk about the vision the more real it seems. If it becomes real to enough people, then it's real. You've done it. Point. Game. Set. And match.

Of course, if all it took to build and sustain a captivating and compelling vision was talk, everyone would do it. But it also takes patience, hard work, perseverance, and salesmanship. That's the challenge. Don't you love it?

There is no pat formula for vision building, but there are some insider secrets that can make it easier. Here's an easy-to-swallow capsule summary of the best thinking on how to create a vision that motivates and moves people and how to keep that vision alive over time:

• No one can impose their vision on others. Yet only a shared vision is a viable vision. Anything less is merely a fantasy. If you are the only one who has the dream, it's not really a dream at all. It's a hallucination.

It takes educating, influencing, motivating, coaching, and modeling to inspire others to buy into your vision (share your dream). Fortunately, these are things effective school leaders do best.

It may help to know that you don't have to get everyone on board before a vision can kick in and begin driving the organization. That may never happen. But a mere critical mass will do.

Eventually, most people will come around, albeit kicking and screaming in some cases. A few may never get with the program. That's OK. It's all right to leave some people behind. It happens every time a new journey is begun.

• Think big enough. Your school doesn't have to settle for being a good school. It can be a great school. Sometimes being good enough isn't good enough.

Some schools become seduced by their own competence. They are good at what they do, so they keep on doing it. And they remain only good when they could be even better. Why stop short of being the best?

As some wag once said, "never let it rest until your good is better and your better is best." You may only get one chance to help conceive a vision for your school's future. Do it right. ("Do it big or stay in bed."—Unknown)

• Back up your vision. Have a personal mission statement, an educational platform, and some well-developed plans in place.

Think through all the issues. Dare to dig into details. Anticipate questions and have ready-made responses. Most people will align with a leader who has a well-thought-out plan.

• Act like a great school even before you become one. Reality has been known to follow pretext.

• Engage others, especially students, to help promote the school's promise. Following are three ideas that have worked well for some of your counterparts:

1.   Have students make a chain with each link representing something good about the school.

2.   Sponsor a student slogan contest based on school values.

3.   Encourage students to design a mural (mosaic) reflecting what the school stands for. Better yet, make the mural a traveling display throughout the community.

• Stick to it. Don't back off. Live by Jeffrey J. Fox's admonition, "Don't give in. Don't let up. Don't let the idea killers whittle you into mediocrity. Think boldly. Execute enthusiastically. Battle the inertia."

• That's what the Marvy's company in Minnesota has done. It's the last company in the entire country still making old-fashioned barber poles—the striped kind. Marvy's made a conscious decision to keep making the poles even though it meant losing money on them and relying on other products to subsidize their manufacture. They did it because nostalgia is part of their mission.
That's putting vision first. Would you do it?

• Institutionalize the vision as much as possible. Have the school board formally adopt it. Incorporate it into your letterhead and make it a part of the performance review process.

• Keep your vision organic. It should evolve and grow or it may get moldy.
The soaring eagle that carries you to greater and greater heights today can become an albatross around your neck weighing you down tomorrow if it doesn't adapt to changing needs and circumstances.
The purpose of a vision is to help invent the future, not to redesign the past.

It's obvious from this advice that nurturing a shared vision for your school can be a great deal of trouble. But it can be a whole lot more trouble trying to run a school without one.

If it would help you to have a personal testimonial to the value of a vision, I'll give you one. As I look back, the two most exciting and fulfilling episodes in my entire career involved organizations driven by an inspirational vision.

One was as part of a team committed to developing a different kind of high school—one where every student was known as an individual, not a number, and no one fell through the cracks. And the second was while working for a district striving to become a "new millennium school system" years before the turn of the century.

In both instances, I never worked harder, achieved more, had more fun, or felt better about it. Vision works. Take my word for it.

Paul O'Neill, former U.S. Treasury secretary and former CEO of Alcoa, says, "Every institution is capable of greatness." That includes your school. But what O'Neill fails to add is that it won't happen unless someone first dreams of making the organization great. That could be you.

If the dream is gone from your school, the only thing left is hard work. How motivating and exciting is that? If you accept the challenge of being an effective school leader, it's your job to bring the dream back. Your students, teachers, parents, and community deserve nothing less.

Is all this talk about vision hogwash? Absolutely not! Every school everywhere needs a passionate leader with a clear image of a better tomorrow starting today. This is my vision. And I'm sticking to it.

W Work and Play

I tried relaxing, but—I don't know—I feel more comfortable tense.

—Cartoon by Hamilton

. . . the purpose of your life is not to serve your business, but the primary purpose of your business is to serve your life.

—Michael E. Gerber
business magnate

It is possible to build a great company and build a great life.

—Jim Collins
Good to Great

Great leaders know how to play. Period. There are no exceptions. But don't school leaders work extremely hard? Of course. Do they work too hard? Probably. Should they play more? Absolutely.

Look closely. The principals and superintendents you admire and want to emulate don't just strive to balance work and play. They actually do it. They live a balanced life.

The best administrators understand that whatever makes them a well-rounded person, makes them a better leader at the same time. They've learned what my former superintendent and mentor Carl Holmstrom taught me early on: "You work to live, not live to work."

It's true. Your job is not your life. Unless you give it permission to be.

Leadership is hard work. But that doesn't mean you have to work all the time—or even that you always have to work longer and harder than everyone else. What it means is that you have to work smarter and make all your time at work really count.

Don't be confused. Workaholism isn't leadership. It's not even a substitute for leadership. And it's not harmless. It's a disease. It even has its own 12-step program.

Workaholism is a corrosive force that can ruin your health, alienate your family, and damage morale and productivity on the job. It has nothing to do with leadership.

Workaholic administrators do too much, expect too much, demand too much, control too much, worry too much, and stay at school or the office too much. It's no wonder they are more likely to burn out than most people. And, of course, it's no surprise, workaholics don't have much fun. ("All work and no play makes Jack . . ."—well, you know.)

Worse yet, workaholism, like alcoholism, is both a family disease (An absentee or preoccupied workaholic makes a lousy spouse and parent.) and a dead-end disease. For some, it can be fatal. For many, it might as well be terminal.

When the job is all consuming, there is no time or energy left to experience, enjoy, strive for, or dream about anything else. Most workaholics exist. They seldom really live. So why do they do it?

Some principals and superintendents work too hard and play too little because they think that's what they're supposed to do; or because they're afraid not to. Some fear that if they aren't always on the job, people will find out they are not indispensable. ("The graveyard is full of indispensable men."—Charles De Gaulle)

Others overwork because it puffs them up and makes them feel superior, important, and self-righteous. But being the Panjandrum of the school doesn't make them the real leader of the school.

Whatever the reason, workaholism is not the pathway to respected leadership. A better route is a well-rounded life. You can't go wrong balancing work and play and the other components of a complete life (e.g., family, friends, wellness, spirituality, and service to the community). That's what your heroes in the profession do.

If you are one of the many school officials who do too much (You know the symptoms: working on weekends, bringing work home every night, missing family functions, skipping vacations), these are steps to "recovery" that have salvaged many workaholics. They can help put some balance back in your life as well. Consider the following.

• Take a tip from AA—"Let go." Delegate. Turn things over. Say "No." Do your own work, not everyone else's. Take the Serenity Prayer to heart:

God, grant me the serenity to accept the things I cannot change, courage to change the things I can, and wisdom to know the difference.

See what happens if you don't try to control everything for a little while. You may be pleasantly surprised. AA just might be on to something.

- Set boundaries on how much you will take on, how much time you will spend on each project, and how long you will work each day. Set an alarm. Quit when you said you would. Then see if the building remains standing the next day.

- Schedule leisure, recreation, and family time. Put them on your calendar, daily planner, or electronic organizer. Treat your family as you would a student, parent, or school-board member. Make an appointment with them and keep it.

- Make it a priority to spend time with the people you love and respect doing what you love to do.

- Try going home on time for a week. If the school survives, try it more often.

- Give up on perfection. Not every task needs to be perfect. Some aren't worth the effort. Give each project the time and attention it deserves—and no more.

- Make one change that lightens your load today. And another one tomorrow. Repeat as needed.

- Revisit old passions (e.g., interests, diversions, hobbies, entertainments, and avocations). You'll wonder why you ever let them drift away.

- Reconnect with your spirituality. Try religion again. Go back to church. Set aside a fixed time for daily prayer or meditation. Seek out quietude. ("God is a friend of silence."—Mother Teresa)

- Apply multitasking to help balance your life (e.g., as a *family*, volunteer with a *church* group to assist at a *community* homeless shelter).

- Take your vacations—every year. And insist that your assistants do, too. No one gives out trophies for passing up vacation opportunities.

If these strategies aren't enough to put balance back into your life, consider getting a personal coach to help sort out your priorities. Do whatever it takes. It's worth it. If you don't get your life right the first time, there is no instant replay.

Of all these measures, the vacation is often the touchiest for school executives. It may just be the best place to start to put work and play in perspective.

Vacations are for taking. Not ignoring. That's why most European countries enforce mandatory 4- to 6-week annual vacation time for everyone.

But in the United States, school leaders—particularly secondary principals and superintendents—like their CEO counterparts in the private sector, are notorious for not using annual vacation time. You may be one of these misguided martyrs.

We've all heard the excuses: We're too busy. I'm in the middle of something. We're short-handed. It's the wrong time. They can't do without me right now. The rationalizations are very familiar. They're also very feeble.

There are plenty of stronger arguments for taking advantage of entitled vacation time, including the following:

- You will actually work better when refreshed and renewed. Even the Energizer Bunny needs recharging sometimes.
- It allows you to get reacquainted with your family.
- Your subordinates need an occasional break from your presence, too.
- It's written into your contract.
- It's fun!

Vacations help prevent burnout. That's why many businesses are now requiring executives to take their allotted vacations. Some school boards have considered similar steps.

Vacations also boost productivity. Even the most fertile fields yield greater harvests if they are allowed to rest periodically. It works for people, too. ("It is well to lie fallow for awhile."—Martin F. Tupper)

Of course, some school leaders take fake vacations. The American Heritage Dictionary defines a vacation as "a period of time devoted to pleasure, rest, or recreation." How many principals and superintendents do you know who stay away from work for a few days or weeks, but spend the time doing everything except relaxing or having fun? It's not just how much time is taken off; it's how the time off is used.

If you seriously want to balance work and play, the following tips can help you "do vacation right" and make your time off work for you:

- *Take vacation for the right reasons.* Take time off for yourself, not for others.

- *Adopt a "vacation attitude."* Think like a retiree, a tourist, or a guest in your own home.

- *Have reasonable expectations.* Vacations don't have to be unforgettable, only renewing.

- *Keep it simple.* Don't get caught-up in overly elaborate plans.

• *Practice moderation.* Don't eat, drink, or do too much. You know it's been a counterproductive vacation if you go back to work feeling worse or more tired than when you took off.

• *Make a clean break.* Don't bring work home. Don't call the office every day. Lock up your laptop. Even make it a little difficult for people at school to get hold of you.

• *Don't swap work on the job for work at home.* (Unless playing handyman is how you have fun.)

• *Get physical.* Be active. A little sensible exercise will make you feel better physically and mentally.

• *Put yourself first.* Do what you want to do, not just what everybody else wants you to do.

• *Do different things and do things differently.* Vacations are opportunities to flex the other side of your brain.

• *Take some risks.* Remind yourself (and others) that you can still be daring.

• *Live in the moment.* Don't fret over the past or future. Savor the present.

• *Spend time with nature.* Go someplace where you can't see concrete for a while. You'll be surprised how healing and restoring it can be.

• *Take off enough time.* You don't want to rush to get everything in. Hurrying is stressful.

• *Keep a record.* Take photos or videos. Make a scrapbook or keep a journal. It will allow you to relive precious memories and moments over and over again.

• *Have fun.*

Skipping vacations won't make you a better leader. Feeling rested and relaxed, being exposed to different experiences, gaining new perspectives, and feeling good about yourself and your family will. Vacations are an investment you shouldn't pass up.

Popular author James Patterson explains that life is like juggling five balls—work, family, friends, health, and integrity. Only work is a rubber ball. If dropped, it will bounce back. The others, however, are glass and will nick or shatter if dropped. Successful leaders have to know how to keep all five balls in the air at once.

To be the best leader you can be, live life intentionally, not by default. Robert Fulghum was right—we really did learn everything we need to know in kindergarten, such as, "learn some and think some and paint and sing and dance and play and work every day some," It works in kindergarten. And it can work in your life.

I learned this lesson well several years ago when a consultant asked our school business manager, "What will your children say about you?" After some reflection, the hardworking financial officer answered, "He was always at the office."

Is that the legacy you want to leave as a leader and as a human being? I don't think so.

So do your job, lead wisely and well—but most important, "play and work every day some!"

 # X-Ray
Thinking

. . . think for yourself and act accordingly . . . ; avoid so far as possible drifting with the current of the mob or being too easily influenced by the outward manifestation of things. Take your own look beneath the surface and don't trust others to look for you.

—Frank B. Jewett

Pulitzer Prize–winning author Ernest "Papa" Hemingway is credited with saying, "The most essential gift for a good writer is a built-in, shock-proof shit detector." He could just as well have been talking about what's essential in a good leader.

One gift all leaders need now more than ever is "X-ray thinking ability"—the capacity to cut through pretenses, defenses, exaggerations, and outright lies to figure out what's really going on and what needs to be done next.

Just as X-rays penetrate solid materials to reveal what's behind or inside, principals and superintendents must see through psychobabble, hype, excuses, false promises, and the con artistry of kids to uncover underlying issues and concerns. If you can't sort out substance from fluff and other stuff, you can't provide a clear direction for others.

As leader of your school, you had better do more than just think fast and straight. You have to think about the right things and think them through. X-rays aren't easily deflected. Your reasoning shouldn't be either. It's harder than you think.

That may be why we hear a lot more today about multitasking (thinking or doing several things simultaneously) than about X-ray thinking. In kaleidoscopic times, multitasking can be a useful skill, but it doesn't always work very well.

Research at Carnegie Mellon University and elsewhere has pretty well established that, where complex issues are involved, the human brain is built to handle one at a time. When people try to think about or do two things at once, neither one is handled very successfully. Two half-baked thoughts don't equal one solid idea.

Multitasking may be a necessary evil of the times. But it doesn't solve real problems in the real world. That takes full attention and concentration (X-ray thinking).

These are the kinds of traits that intrigue Homer Moyer, Jr., a successful Washington, D.C. attorney, who has developed something that may be more useful than the time-honored SAT (Scholastic Aptitude Test). It's called the RAT (Real-world Aptitude Test) and purports to measure "street smarts" and survival skills that give students (and adults) an edge in real life. Moyer is now planning to develop different forms of the RAT for different groups. If there ever is a RAT for school administrators, it will have to yield an X-Ray Thinking Score.

There is no question that the capacity to screen out extraneous information and hone in on real issues is increasingly important in the complex real world of school leadership today. The examples are all around you—if you're paying attention. Here are two cases in point:

Case One

When Lawrence, Kansas, opened a second junior high school featuring a controversial design and a nontraditional program, Superintendent Carl Knox had to pick just the right principal. All signs pointed to selection of the district's most radical and "cutting-edge" administrator. Supporters of the school lobbied for his appointment. Even the superintendent's own cabinet endorsed the selection.

Instead, Knox chose a veteran leader known for being cautious, conventional, and dependable. Knox realized that radical leadership would only polarize the community and create one more hurdle for the new school to overcome. He saw what others didn't—that established and respected leadership would bring enough credibility to the school to give it a chance to succeed. That's X-ray thinking.

It worked. The principal grew into the job, and the school thrived with minimal controversy.

Case Two

When a proposed new staff development program in St. Louis Park, Minnesota, met with strong staff skepticism and resistance before it ever got off the drawing board, putting the right person in charge became crucial.

Everyone on staff assumed that the curriculum director would get the call. It was only logical. And consistent with past practice. But no one told Superintendent Carl Holmstrom that he had to be logical or tradition-bound.

To everyone's surprise, Holmstrom chose the district's chief information and public relations officer to head up the program. He realized that to succeed, it didn't need more of the same old leadership. It needed someone in charge who knew how to communicate effectively, sell new ideas, and change people's minds. Holmstrom's reasoning wasn't conventional, but it was X-ray thinking.

As it turned out, the public relations person proved to be a popular choice, and the staff education program became a hit—even with the hard-core skeptics.

These are typical illustrations of X-ray thinking in action. You can come up with many more. They aren't hard to find. They occur everyday in a school near you. Hopefully, you won't ever have to look beyond your own school to find them.

We all know that X-rays pick up things that are concealed and often go unnoticed. So do successful leaders. The best-ever principals and superintendents are able to cut to the heart of complicated matters and to see what really needs fixing and how to fix it. They do it by remaining relentlessly focused and refusing to allow themselves to be thrown off track.

The problem is that it's more difficult to focus attention than to divide it up and spread it around. Leaders aren't born with X-ray thinking ability. They develop it. You can, too. In fact, you can't afford not to. When you are ready to try, the following tips and exercises can make it easier:

• Take time to think. Some administrators believe that thinking isn't real work. So they don't do much of it. The truth is that thinking is every leader's real work.

• Forget the past. The kind of thinking that led to past success won't necessarily lead to future successes. Be fresh every morning. Face every issue or problem as if you'd never seen anything like it before.

- Be realistic. Face the truth. See things the way they are, not the way you want them to be or they ought to be.

- Know what you don't know.

- Surround yourself with independent thinkers. Don't clone yourself. Hire divergent people—especially teachers and fellow administrators—who will challenge your thinking, not just mirror your thoughts. You don't need "yes" men and women on your staff. You need "yes—but" people.

- Try to look at things from the inside. How does the situation look to the students involved? To the staff members? To parents? To the public?

- Dare to be naïve—even childlike. Kids come up with the damnedest things. So do creative leaders.

- Be prepared. Good ideas can come from anywhere any time. Look for them. It helps to get away from the school sometimes and to talk to new people about old problems now and then.

In his book *A Great Idea*, Charles (Chic) Thompson lists the 10 most idea-friendly situations:

1. While reading.
2. While commuting.
3. In church.
4. During boring meetings.
5. While exercising.
6. While shaving or showering.
7. In the bathroom.
8. In the middle of the night.
9. While performing manual labor
10. Right before going to sleep or just after waking up.

Pay attention. Be ready to receive and accept good ideas wherever and whenever you find them.

- Always write down promising ideas. It's the only way to own your thoughts. You might be surprised how many business and school leaders keep a pen by the bed, a notepad in the car, and a grease pencil in the shower.

- Don't just accept the words you hear or read. Look for feelings and meanings behind the words.

- Always look for the second right answer.

- Don't always think first of yourself and how you are affected. Think outward, not inward.

• Don't think too small. ("We are all at risk any moment to be less than we might be."—Noah ben Shea)

• Remember "Ochman's Razor": Between two competing ideas, the simplest is the preference.

• Use questions to trigger innovative thinking. Keep asking. ("The answer to any problem 'pre-exists.' We need to ask the right questions to reveal the answers." —Jonas Salk)

• Know the differences between revocable and irrevocable deadlines.

• Lacking any better strategy, follow the classic 10-point decision-making process:

1. Identify the issue.

2. Frame the question.

3. Clarify subissues or problem components.

4. Identify multiple options.

5. Narrow the possibilities.

6. Test the most promising courses of action.

7. Pick a preferred solution.

8. Try it out.

9. Assess results.

10. Adopt, modify, or reject the solution. If necessary, repeat the process.

• Be leery of conventional wisdom. It's conventional because it's easy.

• Use metaphors to make sense of changing conditions.

• Don't live and die by data alone. Facts can be manufactured, manipulated, misinterpreted, and misrepresented. Even "scientific proof" isn't infallible.

My favorite scientific proof story is about "Remarkable Mark" who drove a truck for a living and, consequently, was subject to unannounced, random drug tests. Because Mark was a regular drug user, his job and his freedom were constantly at risk. He got around the threat, however, simply by concealing a vial of bleach taped to his leg at all times.

Whenever he was called on to give a urine sample, Mark would go into the restroom, add a little bleach to his urine and turn in a sample containing no trace of illegal substances. He literally had documented evidence that he wasn't using. It worked for a long time. So much for scientific proof.

- Trust your instincts. Let your subconscious do some of your X-ray thinking for you.

There are intuitive ways of knowing things. All effective leaders subconsciously tap into lessons learned from observation or experience. ("The ability to intuit—perceive things without conscious reasoning—is a skill that leaders have long accessed but seldom acknowledged as a sound approach for collecting, analyzing, filtering and applying data."—Karen Dyer and Jacqueline Corothers, *The Intuitive Principal*)

- Don't always take "No" (or "Yes") for an answer. Look deeper.

- Value second thoughts.

- Think long term. Extrapolate the ultimate outcomes of your acts.

- If you have trouble weighing alternatives, try using a Decision-Making Balance Sheet (see example).

Decision-Making Balance Sheet

Suggested Course of Action

Pros	Cons
Short Term:	Short Term:
1.	1.
2.	2.
3.	3.
Long Term:	Long Term:
1.	1.
2.	2.
3.	3.
Weighing Factors:	* Important
	** Somewhat Important
	*** Very Important

- Be open to better ideas. You don't have a monopoly on truth.

- Don't ignore an elephant in the living room. Out of discretion, discomfort, embarrassment, timidity or sheer cowardice, some administrators pussyfoot around delicate issues or subjects (e.g., an employee's drinking problem or widespread student drug use).

Even though the issue is huge and everyone knows about it, they act as if the situation doesn't exist—how dumb is that?

Ignoring problems never solves them and precludes rational thought. Face facts. Admit to yourself and others what's really going on. Deal with touchy topics head-on. It's a leader's way.

Each of the suggestions above will strengthen your X-ray thinking skill. Together, they make a plan. Use it. Put it to work for you. You will notice a difference.

It's important, because X-ray thinking—the ability to sift through sensory overload to zero in on what's true and wise—isn't just something you read about in leadership books. It's what successful principals and superintendents do every day.

Some wannabe leaders and pretenders may try to rely on hocus pocus. Real leaders just focus. They keep the main thing the main thing no matter what. There is no substitute for persistent attention and concentration. Remember, the opposite of being focused is being scatterbrained.

The Roman satirist Petronius had it right when he exhorted, "Uno loco consistit" (stick to one thing). The old advice still rings true. It's the way the leaders you admire and respect think things through.

Obviously, not all school administrators and leaders in other fields are X-ray thinkers. Only the best. That's where you want to be.

Think about it. Now, hold that thought.

Y Yin and Yang

The test of a first-rate intelligence is the ability to hold two opposed ideas in mind at the same time.

—F. Scott Fitzgerald
novelist

The reverse side also has a reverse side.

—Japanese proverb

If you think yin and yang are just names for a cuddly pair of pandas, you're not alone. Most school administrators are not overly familiar with Chinese cosmology, which holds that *yin* (the feminine cosmic principle in nature) combines with *yang* (the masculine principle) to produce all that is and will come to be. They don't teach this stuff in graduate school administration courses.

If they did, you would know that according to ancient Chinese wisdom, yin is exhibited in darkness and cold, while yang is exhibited in light and heat (the sun). They are opposites. And because the Chinese see the world through a dualistic philosophy, they believe that both yin and yang exist in all elements of nature and of life.

If, like most of your peers, you don't know much about Chinese philosophy or yin and yang, you probably don't care. But you should. After all, you work in a world of opposites every day.

If there is one thing every school leader has plenty of, it is contradictions. How many times do you deal with conflicting polarities, diametrically opposite viewpoints, oxymorons, double talk, hidden agendas, dichotomies, seemingly irreconcilable differences, or mutually exclusive alternatives? That many times, huh?

It seems that every day as a principal or superintendent is a paradigm of paradoxes. It's enough to drive you crazy. Or to make you into an effective school leader.

The truth is that if you cannot accommodate opposites, reconcile differences, and mesh diversity into strength, you may not lose your job; but you won't get the job done either.

As it turns out, managing yin and yang is a trade secret among the best leaders in all fields. The trick is to be flexible, adaptable, versatile, inclusive, and eclectic.

And it all starts by exchanging an "either–or" mentality for a "both–and" attitude. Good leaders know how to yin, how to yang, and when to which.

If you need an example of yin and yang in action, look to Bob Weinstein, a popular business and technical writer, who has identified key differences between male and female CEOs. (It's not much of a stretch to assume that similar differences exist between male and female school administrators.)

According to Weinstein, men and women executives share the same broad goals but employ different (opposite) leadership strategies and styles.

Male CEOs tend to work as a team, are more decisive, decide more quickly, follow their hunches, and don't agonize over matters too long. Although fewer in number, female executives are more likely to go it alone, look at the big picture, and worry over decision making for a longer period of time.

What Weinstein doesn't point out, however, is that the very best CEOs (male and female) don't stick exclusively to any one style. They work both sides (opposite sides) of the street. They mix and match and use whatever works. Yes—you saw it coming—the best school leaders do the same thing.

If you want to play in the same league with the super stars of school leadership, you need to learn

- When to "kick butt" (yang) and when to hug (yin).

- When to be decisive (yang) and when to take it slow (yin).

- When to give orders (yang) and when to listen (yin).

- When to set boundaries (yang) and when to encourage autonomy (yin).

- When to be macho (yang) and when to be maestro (yin).

- When to manage (yang) and when to lead (yin). ("Increasingly, the people who are most effective are those who essentially are both managers and leaders."—David Thomas, founder of Wendy's).

- When to applaud performance and when to give nonperformers what legendary football coach George Halas calls a "standing boo."

The leadership style of choice for the most successful CEOs, principals, and superintendents is "situational"—whatever circumstances call for. The sooner you learn this, the quicker you can become a better school leader.

A+ team leaders refuse to be bothered by forces that pull them in opposite directions. They realize that there will always be some dynamic tension between headquarters (district administration) and field offices (individual schools) and between various stakeholders, participants, and constituents. It's that way in all organizations.

This simply means it is the leader's role to channel the energy of opposing forces in the direction of mutually acceptable goals (e.g., when teacher unions join forces with school boards to pass referendums for increased funding).

Skill in managing opposites doesn't come easily, but it can be learned or developed. The following specific measures and advice are designed to widen your thinking and stretch your leadership style to better accommodate contradictions. (Some of these suggestions may seem a little strange or make you uncomfortable, but they will work. Of course, you will never know unless you try them.)

1. Realize that things are not always what they seem to be. Take a second look—and then a closer look.

2. Make a habit of doing the opposite of what's normally expected (e.g., invite kids to faculty meetings to air gripes about staff members instead of vice versa or show up at bus stops to give drivers kudos instead of complaints).

3. Don't always automatically accept the first or most obvious answer.

4. Practice reframing. Flip-flop the way you look at things. Don't ask what you can do; ask what you can't do. Change positive statements into negative ones—and negative statements into positives. Look not only at what the problem is, but what it is not.

Don't just ask, "What's wrong with them?" Ask, "What's wrong with me?" Look not just at what the curriculum is, but what it isn't. By seeing what is not happening, you just might uncover what ought to happen.

That's exactly the way the Japanese captured a major share of the U.S. automobile market in the '70s and '80s. They saw what Detroit wasn't doing—making small, economical cars—and then did it. Who knows? Reframing may put you onto something equally as big.

5. Look for trends in the making. Try to spot when things will start going in an opposite direction.

6. Look for creative organizational ideas and policy solutions in unusual places (e.g., churches and theater groups).

7. Work puzzles, cryptograms, and logic problems to build skill for thinking in different ways.

8. Try some "lateral thinking." First introduced by management trainer and author Edward de Bono this process offers an alternative to traditional linear (step-by-step) problem solving. The technique calls for allowing irrelevant ideas (even random nouns plucked from the dictionary) to intrude into your thinking process and then mentally playing around with any and all possible connection(s) the orphan ideas may have to the original problem.

Sometimes unintentional, disconnected, off-the-wall ideas can generate creative and unusual solutions. Lateral thinking works like intuition, but is more systematic. Sound crazy? Successful business leaders around the world have used Bono's approach to unblock creativity and steer corporate thinking in new or opposite directions. Who's to say it won't work for you?

9. Trigger the opposite side of your brain. Try using the less dominant hand (e.g., for writing or eating). It worked for Ben Franklin and Leonardo da Vinci.

If your left hemisphere is dominant, try painting, drawing, singing, or dancing. If your right brain usually dominates, work with statistics or construct a scaled model. You may be surprised at the results.

10. Look beyond the obvious. Look for new, unnoticed, or hidden patterns or connections.

11. Try "reverse visioning." Pretend you are 90 years old. Look back at your life and answer these questions:

- What did you do with your life? What was missing?
- What would you change or do differently? Why? How?
- When were you really right? When were you dead wrong?
- When was the other guy right and you were wrong? Why didn't you see it?
- When did the exact opposite happen than what you anticipated or predicted? How did that happen?

- How will you be remembered? What will it say on your tombstone? What should be the title of your memoirs?
- What are your most pleasant memories? Most unpleasant?
- What were the significant milestones or turning points in your life?
- What were your top five accomplishments?
- What will your children say about your life?

Seeing your life from another angle can reveal unexpected possibilities.

12. Change your location to gain an opposite perspective. It can make a huge difference. (Just imagine how differently things looked depending on which side of the street you were standing and watching when Lady Godiva made her famous ride.)

Do more MWWA (Managing While Walking Around). It's an easy, physical way to change what you see and, sometimes, what you think.

13. When people behave strangely, don't automatically assume they are crazy. Look for reasons and causes behind the behavior. They may be a lot saner than you think. (Remember Aronson's First Law: "People who do crazy things are not necessarily crazy. Sometimes, the social situation is so powerful that an overwhelming majority of ordinary people behave in a strange manner."—Elliot Aronson, social psychologist)

14. Refuse to be surprised when the opposite thing happens.

15. Reverse your routine. Start with the activity you normally do last and work backward through the day.

16. Allow for serendipity. Often luck or chance will reveal the opposite of what you expect.

17. Learn from children. They're not bothered by opposites.

These exercises and experiences will heighten your awareness of different ways of seeing and doing things and of differing paths leading to identical results. The goal is a more free, uninhibited, unbiased, and open mind-set as a leader—what Charles (Chic) Thompson calls a state of "naïve incubation."

Successful leaders in all occupations see opposites and know how opposites work. They understand that to lead, you must know how to follow and that to prosper, you must be frugal. That's the way it is in business. That's the way it is in life. And that's the way it is in your school.

Being an effective school leader is getting more complicated all the time. And more confusing. About the only thing that works for sure anymore is to accept the simultaneous existence of opposites and to see the truth of both sides. (There is always plenty of truth to go around.)

That's why you have to learn to live with contradictions. Better yet, become a contradiction yourself when necessary.

The difference between a very fine school and a truly great school isn't in the curriculum or in the organizational structure or in the per pupil expenditures. It's in the leadership.

Principals and superintendents who adopt a yin style can run good schools. And administrators who use a yang approach can run good schools. But it's the leaders who integrate both strategies who run the recognized, head-and-shoulders-above-the-rest, *great* schools.

But how can a leader be both yin and yang? Just follow Lao-tzo's advice, "Learn to see things backward, inside out, and upside down." Sound like silly advice? It's really just the opposite.

Z | Zen for School Leaders

The basic principle in Zen is the same everywhere. Like Mount Fuji, there are different paths to the summit.

—Kusho Itabashi, abbot
Soji monastery in Yokahama

Zen . . . does not confuse spirituality with thinking about God while one is peeling potatoes. Zen spirituality is just to peel the potatoes.

—Alan Watts
author

If there is a Zen of business, this would be it: "Solutions are problems and problems are solutions." There is no problem that can't be solved and no solution that can't become a problem.

—Dale Danten, columnist
"The Corporate Curmudgeon"

A little Zen can make you a better school leader. No, reader, I haven't gone all goofy, weird, or metaphysical on you. But I know a good deal when I see one.

Good leaders welcome real-world resources and practical tools wherever they find them, and Zen has something to offer that you may not get anywhere else.

Like alternative medicine and other forms of Eastern wisdom and Asian philosophy, Zen is becoming increasingly popular in the United States and Europe—even among practical-minded, bottom-line business leaders.

Proponents claim that Zen is a rare voice of sanity because it offers a different way of seeing the world based on rediscovering who we are and seeing life as it really is. They claim that Zen provides something that is missing in Western culture—something that most school leaders could use a lot more of.

And you don't have to become a convert, study under a Zen master, or practice any Zen rituals to get it. But you do have to understand a little bit about what Zen is. You may be surprised.

For starters (especially for those concerned about separation of church and state), Zen isn't exactly a religion. It is more about the human mind than about God. Zen is a form of Buddhism that emphasizes the value of meditation and intuition.

Zen is an abbreviation of Zenna, which means collectness of mind (meditative absorption). It is both a collection of teachings and a set of practices that fuse philosophy, spirituality, and art.

A Zen mind-set stresses inner serenity, connectedness, enlightenment, clarity that comes from within, and being present in the moment. Some scholars say that Zen is just your ordinary, everyday life. That doesn't sound so weird, does it?

Some Westerners are surprised to find out that the basic precepts of Zen are much the same as those of any other religion you might choose (see examples).

Zen Precepts

3 Pure Precepts

1. Refrain from evil.
2. Do only good (inner life)
3. Do good for others.

10 Great Precepts

1. Do not kill.
2. Do not steal.
3. Do not covet.
4. Do not tell untruths.
5. Do not spread delusions.
6. Do not speak ill of others.
7. Do not be proud and devalue others.
8. Do not be ungenerous.
9. Do not be angry.
10. Do not be defensive.

—Sound familiar?—

If you need further evidence that a Zen perspective can be an effective tool for mainstream school leaders, consider these characteristics:

• Zen is grounded in the here and now. It focuses on the immediacy of the present moment and the opportunities it offers.

• Zen has a sense of self-deprecating humor.

• The Zen philosophy is both practical and spiritual.

• The key words in the language of Zen include spontaneity, joy, tranquility, discovery, and focus.

• The most important Zen qualities are Great Faith, Great Courage, and Great Inquiry.

• Self-reliance is the core of Zen teaching.

• Zen practice is based on the art of focusing—a skill that can carry over into everyday life.

• The goal of Zen is clarity and enlightenment (e.g., to strip away the "mental pudding" of life).

• Zen promotes simplicity of life and compassion for self and others.

• Zen teaches through paradoxical statements and puzzling parables called *koans*. Not surprisingly, the ultimate *koan* is life itself.

Does all this sound interesting? It should. These principles add up to an attitude and frame of reference that can support and enhance all forms of leadership—especially school leadership.

You don't have to be Buddhist to benefit from the lessons of Zen. You just have to want to do a better job for your school. If you internalize and act on the following Zen teachings, you may not achieve a state of Nirvana (an ideal condition of wisdom, compassion, harmony, and joy), but you will be a more effective principal or superintendent.

• Live in the moment.
• Be spontaneous.
• Ignore negativity.
• Pay attention to the experience at hand.
• Value the wonder of life.
• Be joyful.
• Be self-reliant.
• Don't waste words.

- Be compassionate.
- Seek self-knowledge.
- Experience and honor nature.
- Appreciate simplicity.
- Take time to meditate.

These lessons alone should be worth several graduate credits in school leadership. But only if you actually put them into practice in your school. It's not that difficult.

A good place to start is by applying the Japanese concept of a "visual workplace" to your school through the use of the popular Feng Shui or "Image Management" (manipulating elements in the work environment to achieve the desired image, such as friendliness and welcoming). To the Japanese, the primary components of an effective visual workplace are organization, orderliness, cleanliness, and discipline.

Space isn't passive. Appearance, arrangement, and even color can create moods, influence behavior and facilitate desired actions. Businesses have known this all along. For years, grocery stores, restaurants, and department stores have arranged, furnished, and decorated space to help achieve desired goals (in this case, sales and profit). Schools can—and should—do the same thing.

If you could create an environment (e.g., classrooms, offices, lounges—anywhere and everywhere that people study, learn, work, and play) that makes everyone in your school feel better and do better, why wouldn't you? You can. Zen can help.

Some of your colleagues have already figured this out. Have you noticed how the best schools look? What image do they project?

Are they energized by plants and artwork? Super illuminated to create a sense of spaciousness and friendliness? Made to feel more comfortable by displays of magazines, use of aquariums, and provisions for privacy? Kept exceptionally clean and well maintained? (Most people are uncomfortable in messy or disorganized spaces. That's why some schools encourage student organizations to "adopt" a hallway or playground area to help keep litter-free.)

If the answer to all of these questions is yes, it's Zen at work. It can work for you, too.

The best example may be in something as simple as color selection. Most schools today are either institutional gray or "blah" off-white. There's a better way.

Did you know that dark blue is powerful? That yellow is weak? Beige is neutral? And red is intimate? There's a reason why repeated retail research shows that blue suits outsell brown suits, no matter who is wearing them.

Smart leaders don't pick colors because they are pretty or practical or cheap. They pick them because they work. For example, most color experts agree that shades of blue work best in reception areas, because they are soothing, and white and dark blue with a touch of red is the best color scheme for offices. You should know about this.

Of course, a Zen approach can help you with more than color. Its attention to detail covers shapes and other characteristics as well. It's a good thing, because even the size and shape of your school's logo or the font on your Web site can be important.

Zen stresses simplicity, sparseness, naturalness, and harmony in furnishings and decorations. It's a way of thinking that can make all the spaces in your school work for you, not against you.

Of course, there are more ways than just managing space to incorporate the best of Zen into your school and into your leadership style. Here's a short list of possibilities to whet your imagination:

• Try playing classical music during study time. Music with a beat slower than the human heart beat has been shown to produce a sense of balance and improve concentration. (Sorry, kids, rock 'n' roll, hip-hop, and rap won't work.)

• Create a silent place within the school where students and adults alike can go for a few moments of peace and serenity in the midst of frenzy. Quietude is an elixir.

• Many parochial schools have the advantage of a chapel on site. It's an idea public schools could well borrow—without the religious trappings.

• If a stubborn problem won't yield an answer, try assigning it to your subconscious for a while. Sometimes, you do your best thinking when you're not thinking about it.

• Have your school designated as a "Peace Site." Erect a "peace pole" as a daily reminder of the school's commitment to compassion and positive relationships between people and nations.

• Learn to laugh at yourself. Do it publicly. Encourage others to do the same.

• Try serving tea to the faculty after school occasionally to help everyone mellow out. It was a tradition at Evanston Township High School (Illinois) for many years.

• Slow down—even when things are most hectic—maybe especially when things are most hectic. Once in a while, it pays to follow Izaak Walton's example, "I have laid aside business, and gone a-fishing . . ."

• Pay attention to your visual reactions (e.g., what makes you tingle, gives you goose bumps, or raises the hair on the back of your neck). It heightens your awareness of what's going on around you.

• Relax more. Most Zen rituals are designed to offer respite from the stress of daily living. If Bill Gates can take time to jump on a trampoline to shake off the tension of the day's ups and downs, you can find your own rituals for relaxation.

• Try out the simplest form of meditation. Just choose an external object and concentrate on it exclusively for 5 to 15 minutes, shoving all other thoughts out of your mind. It's a good way to calm down and get reenergized at the same time.

• Become a little more philosophical. Not everything is a matter of life and death. As my first mentor in graduate school, Oscar Haugh, used to advise us, "Sometimes, stop being a heller and just be a what-the-heller." The Laotian Buddhists have a similar phrase, *Baw pen nyang*, meaning, "So it goes" or "That's life." It's a phrase every principal or superintendent could use more often.

Obviously, a little Zen-like thought and action can be a good thing for any organization—particularly for a school.

All successful leaders—in schools, businesses, or anywhere else—have to be more than hard-driving task masters or fast-acting movers and shakers. They also have to be meditative, introspective, and spiritual at times. (Maybe that's why most successful CEOs don't have MBAs. They have liberal arts degrees instead.)

For years before his death, Bob Terry, director of the leadership center at the famed Hubert H. Humphrey Institute of Public Affairs, preached the need for "reflective leadership"—for leaders who diagnose problems, think before they act, and constantly ask, "What's really happening here?"

As it turns out, Terry was right. That's why this chapter on Zen is included in a book about school leadership.

The circle is a prominent Zen symbol. It represents completeness and unity—no beginning and no end. This is the reason why the book begins with "Attitude" and ends with "Zen." The book has now come full circle. For you see, a Zen-like attitude is another mark of an effective school leader.

A Final Word

With leadership, everything is possible. Without leadership, nothing is possible.

—Paul O'Neill, former U.S.
Treasury Secretary and former Alcoa CEO

That's it. School leadership from A to Z. Is that all there is to it? Absolutely not. Is it a good start? Much better than that.

Learning the alphabet won't make a child a great reader. But it will give that child the basic tools to become one.

This book won't make you Principal or Superintendent-of-the-Year or guarantee your school's success. But it does give you the necessary ingredients. You have to do the sifting, mixing, stirring, and final baking for yourself.

If your school is not what it could or should be, something needs to be changed. But nothing can actually change until the leader changes first. That's you.

When you are ready, use the preceding pages to help you figure out what to change, how to change, and how to score yourself differently. It's never easy, but it's always worth it.

Some administrators just try to make it through the day—every day. But real leaders don't want the day to end and can't wait for the next one to begin—because they know that being a leader is a gift. They know it is important work. They know it is hard work. And they know what former General Electric CEO Jack Welch has said all along—

Being a CEO is the nuts . . .

Kids think learning the alphabet is a blast. Mastering school leadership from A to Z is, too. Successful leaders are successful because they are having a good time. (That's another thing they don't teach you in graduate school.)

So learn your ABCs. Grow all you can. Dream all you can. Do all you can. Be all you can.

And don't forget to have some fun!

Good luck.

Resource 1

A New Vocabulary
for School Leaders

Language affects thinking. Thinking affects behavior. Companies must change how people speak if they are to change how people behave.

—Buckingham and Coffman
First, Break All the Rules

God only knows educators don't need any more jargon. But sometimes a few fresh phrases can shake up stale thinking.

Words are powerful, but they can get tired and overworked. Jargon gets jaded, and buzzwords eventually lose their buzz. That's why a new vocabulary now and then can help provoke and promote new perspectives leading to new actions.

A word is just a word until it is just the right word, then it makes all the difference. New words equal new ways.

Some of the following terms, borrowed from the business community, may be just what you're looking for to jump-start your staff's thinking. Select any that work for you—use them sparingly—and they just may help you build a different and better school.

Alacrity The capability to move from decision to action quickly; promptness in response.

Ambiguity tolerance The ability to live with unsolved problems.

Associates   Everyone in the organization (paid and unpaid) who contributes to its success—without distinction based on hierarchy.

Broadbonding   A pay plan featuring broad, overlapping ranges of pay for each role or job title.

Boundaryless organization   No rigid turf distinctions (e.g., no barriers between departments).

Bureaucratic creep   Incremental growth of bureaucracy and red tape (e.g., rules, regulations, forms, policies, procedures, or overlapping layers of approval or authority).

Blameless errors   Unintentional mistakes that are no one's fault.

Clockroaches   Employees who contribute nothing but still get paid on your time.

Courage to cull   Daring to remove nonperformers.

Differentiation   A business practice of rewarding the best and weeding out the rest.

DQYDJ   Don't quit your day job.

Decision overload   An overdose of choices.

E-noyance   Worthless e-mail messages

Face time   One-on-one conversation.

Gotcha mentality   Structures, rules, and practices designed to catch people doing something wrong.

Hi-po   High potential; may apply to people or programs.

Intellectual capital (human inventory)   An organization's greatest assets (e.g., sensing, judging, creating).

Impression management   Manipulating elements in the environment to create a desired image.

Kaizen Japanese concept of permanent, daily, and continuous improvement.

Kitchen table English Plain talk; no jargon.

Navigation Leading by charting a course, guiding the organization in the right direction, and steering around obstacles.

Occupational half-life The time it takes for knowledge and skills to become obsolete.

Open Book Management (OBM) Opening up the books to all employees; full sharing of financial information.

Ownership attitude All employees think, worry, dream, and act like an owner.

Positive turbulence Freedom to challenge convention and corporate logic.

Pragmatic idealism Dealing with practical problems in a common-sense way while retaining long-range ideals.

Punditocracy Domination by a group of self-appointed experts.

Rocking-chair syndrome Lots of movement without going anywhere.

User-centered Starting with what the worker needs to succeed and working backward from there.

Visual workplace A Japanese concept implying organization cleanliness and orderliness (*see* impression management).

Resource 2

What Business Leaders Say About Leadership That School Leaders Need to Hear

Schools and businesses are different. But leadership is leadership. When successful business leaders talk about leadership, school leaders should listen. There are lessons to be learned.

- "Management is problem-oriented. Leadership is opportunity-oriented. Management works in the system. Leadership works on the system."—Stephen Covey

- "The question, Who ought to lead? is like asking, Who ought to be the tenor in the quartet? Obviously, the man who can sing tenor."—Henry Ford

- "Power flows to the man who knows how."—Elbert Hubbard

- "Anything delayed will get further delayed."—Robert Half, temporary help pioneer.

- "You are your greatest investment."—George Mathews Adams

- "Everything can be improved."—C. W. Barren

- "Progress would be wonderful if it would only stop."—Robert Musil

- "So much for the power and glory of running a large organization. On a good day, it's the best job in the world; on an average day, it's more work than most people will ever understand. And on a bad day? You don't want to know."—Mark McCormack, columnist

- "The boss is the boss . . . And remember: Every boss has a boss."—Stephen Viscusi, business author, advice from his mother.

- "How to Fail
  Try too Hard.
  How to Succeed
  Try Hard Enough."—Malcolm Forbes

- "All technology should be assumed guilty until proven innocent."—David Brower

- "An objective without measurement is like a dieter without a bathroom scale."—David Hotler, manager, The Dynamics Corporation

- "Management is about human beings. Its task is to make people capable of joint performance, to make their strengths effective and their weaknesses irrelevant."—Peter Drucker, 92-year-old management czar

- "If you have a job without aggravation, you don't have a job."—Malcom Forbes

- "Let chaos reign; then rein in chaos."—Andy Grove, chairman, Intel

- "Being Number 1 or Number 2 isn't an objective, it's a requirement."—Jack Welch

- "If you're not keeping score, you're only practicing."—Jan Leschly, CEO, Smith Kline Beecham

- "If you can't measure it, you can't manage it."—Harris and Brannick, *Finding and Keeping Great Employees*

- "Finding a better way every day."—Slogan at General Electric

- "Swipe from the best, then adapt."—Tom Peters

- "We lead by being human. We don't lead by being corporate."—Paul Hawken, cofounder, Smith and Hawken

- "An organization is therefore a structured institution. If it is not structured, it is a mob. Mobs don't get things done, they destroy things."—Theodore Levitt

- "You can work or you can meet—you can't do both."—Peter Drucker

- "Luck, speed and brilliant technology has never been enough because somebody is always luckier, faster and technologically brighter."—Michael E. Gerbe

- "I think the purpose of life is to be useful, to be responsible, to be honorable, to be compassionate. It is, above all, to matter, to count, to stand for something, to have made a difference that you lived at all."—Leo Rosten, immigrant author

- "Today's laurels are tomorrow's compost."—Tom Peters

- "If it has staples, it won't get read."—Old joke among managers

- "A human being should be able to change a diaper, plan an invasion, butcher a hog, design a building, write a sonnet, balance accounts, build a wall, set a bone, comfort the dying, take orders, give orders, cooperate, act alone, solve equations, analyze a new problem, cook a tasty meal, fight efficiently and die gallantly. Specialization is for insects." Robert Heinlen (Whew! Sounds like the definition of a school leader to me.)

- "The highest level of achievement comes from the heart."—Hal Rosenbluth, CEO, Rosenbluth International

- "Success is good management in action."—William E. Holler

- "If you want someone to do a good job, give them a good job to do."—Frederick Herzberg, management theorist

- "Keep strong if possible. In any case, keep cool. Have unlimited patience. Never corner an opponent, and always assist him to save face. Put yourself in his shoes—so as to see things through his eyes. Avoid self-righteousness like the devil—nothing is so self-blinding."—Basil Henry Liddell Art

- "The factory of the future will have only two employees, a man and a dog. The man will be there to feed the dog. The dog will be there to keep the man from touching the equipment."—Warren Bennes, University of Southern California

- "Powerlessness corrupts. Absolute powerlessness corrupts absolutely."—Rosabeth Moss Kantor, Harvard Business School

- "We've got to get really good at thinking about thinking."—Don Winkler, CEO, Ford Motor Credit Company

- "Leaving clarity behind to get speed is abdication."—Matt Kissiner, Pitney Bowes Financial Services

- "Vibrant companies must put together five-year plans. But they must be willing to change their five-year plan every single year. It's the only way to stay alive."—Walt Disney

- "Great managers make it all seem so simple. Just select for talent, define the right outcomes, focus on strengths and then, as each employee grows, encourage him or her to find the right fit. Complete these steps with every single employee and your department will yield perennial excellence. It's almost inevitable."—Marcus Buckingham and Curt Coffman, *First, Break All the Rules*

Resource 3

Business Books You Might Want to Read to Become a Better School Leader

A book is the only place you can examine a fragile thought without breaking it, or explore an explosive idea without fear it will go off in your face.

—Edward G. Morgan
writer

The best leaders are students of leadership. So even business books can be a gold-mine find for good school leaders who want to get better.

Business writers don't just write about profit and loss and strictly business stuff. They write about how to set goals, how to run an efficient organization, achieve results, and get the most out of people. These are subjects all leaders are interested in—that you should be interested in.

That's why some principals and superintendents I know read business best sellers. They know it makes them better school leaders. It might make you a better leader, too. You will never know unless you try. If you are interested, here are a few good resources to start with.

Badaracco, John L. (2002). *Leading Quietly: An Unorthodox Guide to Doing the Right Thing.* Boston, MA: Harvard Business School Press.

Bates, Charles. (1991). *Pigs Eat Wolves.* St. Paul, MN: YES International.

Bennis, Warren G., and Nannus, Burt. (1997). *Leaders: Strategies for Taking Charge.* New York: Harper Business Books.

Bennis, Warren G., and Thomas, Robert. (2002). *Geeks and Geezers: How Era, Values and Defining Moments Shape Leaders.* Boston, MA: Harvard Business School Press.

Blanchard, Ken, and Bankes, Sheldon. (1998). *Gung Ho: Turn on the People in any Organizations.* New York: William Morrow.

Blanchard, Ken, Carlos, John P., and Randolph, Alan. (1996). *Empowerment Takes More Than a Minute.* New York: MJF Books.

Blanchard, Kenneth, and Johnson, Spencer. (1984). *The One-Minute Manager.* New York: William Morrow.

Bossidy, Larry, and Charan, Ram. (2002). *Execution: The Discipline of Getting Things Done.* New York: Crown Business.

Bridges, William. (1991*). Managing Transition: Making the Most of Change.* Reading, MA.: Addison-Wesley.

Buckingham, Marcus, and Coffman, Curt. (1994). *First, Break All the Rules: What the World's Greatest Managers Do Differently.* New York: Simon & Schuster.

Collins, Jim. (2001). *Good to Great: Why Some Companies Make the Leap . . . and Others Don't.* New York: Harper Business.

Cooper, Robert K., and Sawat, Ayman. (1996). *Executive EQ: Emotional Intelligence in Leadership and Organizations.* New York: Grosset and Putnam.

Covey, Stephen R. (1989). *The 7 Habits of Highly Effective People.* New York: Simon and Schuster.

Covey, Stephen R. (1996). *Principle-Centered Leadership.* New York: Simon and Schuster.

Essey, Louellen, and Kusy, Mitchell. (1999). *Fast Forward Leadership: How to Exchange Outmoded Practices for Forward Looking Leadership Today.* New York: Pearson.

Fritz, Robert. (1999). *The Path of Least Resistance for Managers: Designing Organizations to Succeed.* San Francisco: Barrett-Koehler.

Giuliani, Rudolf W. (2002). *Leadership.* New York: Hyperion.

Goleman, David, and Boyatzis, Richard. (2002). *Primal Leadership: Realizing the Power of Emotional Intelligence.* Boston, MA.: Harvard Business Press.

Harris, Jim, and Brannick, Joan. (1999). *Finding and Keeping Great Employees.* New York: Amacom.

Jensen, Bill. (2000*). Simplicity: The New Competitive Edge in a World of More, Bigger, Faster.* Cambridge, MA: Perseus Books.

Jonson, Spencer. (1998). *Who Moved My Cheese? An Amazing Way to Deal With Change in Your Work and in Your Life.* New York: G. P. Putnam's Sons.

Lundin, Stephen, Paul, Harry, and Christensen, John. (2000*). Fish: A Remarkable Way to Boost Morale and Improve Results.* New York: Hyperion.

Nelson, Bob. (1994). *1001 Ways to Reward Employees.* New York: Workman.

Nelson, Bob. (1997). *1001 Ways to Energize Employees.* New York: Workman.

Senge, Peter. (1990). *The Fifth Discipline: The Art and Practice of the Learning Organization.* New York: Doubleday.

Welch, Jack. (2001). *Jack: Straight From the Gut.* New York: Warner Books.

Wheatley, Margaret J. (1999). *Leadership and the New Science: Discovering Order in a Chaotic World.* San Francisco: Berrett-Koehler.

Resource 4

Borrowing From Business

Bright Ideas You Can Use in Your School Starting Tomorrow Morning

The trick—yes, the trick—to sustainability lies, almost entirely, in being obsessed with constant improvement, eventually institutionalizing constant improvement.

—Sara P. Noble
management consultant and editor

Good ideas can come from anywhere, and they don't have to cost big bucks. There is no copyright on genius. That's why the best school leaders I know will steal suggestions from anywhere if it makes their school better.

Unfortunately, businesses are a source of ideas educators often overlook. We tend to think that businesses are playing an entirely different game. We're wrong—or at least only partially correct.

Despite any differences, successful business leaders still have to find effective ways to attract, motivate, inspire, and manage people to get the job done. Their livelihood depends on it. Actually, so does yours.

So don't be too proud to lift a few promising practices and ideas from your business counterparts. It's not heresy. It's not unprofessional. It's called working smarter.

For example, here are some tips and strategies from successful businesses that you may want to consider for use in your school. (They are free for the taking and there's no charge for just looking.)

1. Hold a fishing tournament for employees and their families. It's a new twist on the traditional "company picnic" and can be a lot more fun.

2. You create yearbooks for students. Why not one for the adults in the organization, complete with pictures and information on interests, hobbies, family, and favorite things? It can help staff members connect and get to know each other more personally. Parents will like it, too.

3. When key staff members have to put in a lot of extra time, send flowers and a dinner gift certificate to the employee's family. It's a touch of class that has worked well for Rick Johnson, founder and CEO of Burjon Steel Services in Springboro, Ohio.

4. Set aside an evening to sweep floors with your custodians. It builds rapport and you'll learn a lot. Custodians know everything that's going on in the organization—especially the juicy stuff.

5. Once a year, allow employees to vote on undecided personnel issues, such as tardiness penalties, smoking policies, and dress code. Then make the outcomes part of policy in the official employee handbook. Frederick Shulte, Jr., Delta Land Surveying and Engineering, in Flint, Michigan, vouches for the practice.

6. Distribute pocket notebooks to all employees to write down questions and suggestions. The pages can easily be ripped out and dropped in the school's suggestion box.

7. Clone your best employees by having them recommend future hires.

8. Write your course descriptions, student and parent handbooks, and other communications as if you were writing a letter to a friend. An informal, personal approach always works best.

9. Let employees use the school shop and equipment to work on their own personal woodworking and craft projects on weekends.

10. Try scheduling a weekly two-hour session to "talk to yourself" (time to think). An early morning hour at some location away from the office works best for Neal Patterson, CEO of Cerner Corporation in Kansas City, Missouri.

11. Find out everything you can about the teaching candidates you want to hire the most (e.g., age of children, spouse's work status, special

interests, etc.) to help you figure out the appropriate "dealmaker"—what it will take to bring the candidate on board. (Note: It's often not money.)

12. Don't be afraid to use gimmicks to motivate your staff. For example, the Ridgeway Development Corporation in Atlanta has given employees a mirror with a note attached that read, "Face it . . . you make a difference." Likewise, the Citizens and Southern National Bank in South Carolina has passed out footballs to "Kick off" a new year and tape measures to "measure progress." Where does it say that being corny can't work?

13. Use a lot more ad hoc, self-directed, and cross-functional teams to solve problems and carry out projects. Successful businesses do it all the time. Schools have just scratched the service. It's a good way to break down hierarchies and remove barriers between specialized departments. It also produces results. After all, "None of us is as smart as all of us."

14. Develop a strategy to help you know what to listen for. Simplicity expert Bill Jensen recommends these guideposts:

C—Connection (How is this relevant to what I do?)

L—List of next steps (What do I have to do?)

E—Expectations (What will success look like?)

A—Ability (What resources and support do I need?)

R—Return (What's in it for me–WIIFM?)

15. Put all letters of appreciation, congratulation, and commendation you receive from students, parents, and community members in the appropriate employee's permanent personnel file. Kudos should be kept.

16. If you have an open communication system for sharing information and ideas, showcase it by giving it a name. Employees will be more likely to use it if they know what to call it. The Body Shop calls theirs DODGI—Department of Darned Good Ideas.

17. Hold mini-courses for your customers (parents) on such topics as helping with homework, planning for college, or talking to teens. Home Depot has built a vast reservoir of good will by conducting classes for all its customers (men, women, and even kids). It can pay off for your school as well.

18. Treat applicants like customers. Try to create a positive experience for every applicant, even the ones you don't hire. You never know who or what you will be looking for in the future.

19. Never have enough time? Try arriving 45 minutes earlier and leaving 15 minutes later. It equals an hour a day and gives you an additional month of productive time during the course of a year. It's a practice that has given many successful CEOs an edge.

20. Refuse to panic. Practice taking your time under pressure. You can get better at it. Some leaders suggest that if you have 10 seconds to make a decision, think for a full nine before committing to action.

21. Don't waste precious staff development time trying to teach talent. Many businesses have tried and failed. It can't be done. People have talent or they don't. You can teach information, skills, strategies, and techniques. But you can't put in what's not there to start with.

22. Have candidates write up minutes of their interview with you. Some may reveal information and dimensions not observable during the oral question-and-answer session. And it's a good way to test writing skills at the same time.

23. Issue engraved desktop nameplates to all employees, not just to the top brass. It costs a little, but boosts morale a lot.

24. Pass out kazoos for an impromptu concert to celebrate special events or accomplishments.

25. Schedule a Bring-Your-Pet-to-Work Day for employees. It will generate a lot of conversation, excitement, and fun among staff members. And the kids will love it, too.

26. Implement an employee fitness, health, and wellness initiative (e.g., exercise workouts, back care, and carpel tunnel prevention and ergonomic intervention programs, smoking cessation clinics, and safety awareness classes). Such programs have reduced injuries, medical insurance claims and absenteeism, improved morale, and increased productivity for companies such as Chevron Texaco Corporation and Toyota Motor Manufacturing in Kentucky. This may be too good a deal for your school to pass up. While you're at it, a good spin-off idea is to make the school gym and physical education fitness equipment available to community members—especially senior citizens—for workouts during after school hours.

27. Include the following disclaimer in all staff handbooks: "This is not a binding contract. All content may be modified at any time." This simple language may avoid complex litigation or legal problems later on.

28. When evaluating suggestions, proposals, and new ideas, put halos (circles) around the good ones and coffins (rectangles) around the losers. It has proved to be useful short hand at General Electric.

29. Allow staff members to use some of their planning time to do volunteer work in the community.

30. Limit presentations at staff meetings to seven minutes. Just in case, bring an alarm clock to enforce the time limit.

31. Provide free computer games to help teachers and other staff members overcome high-tech phobia.

32. Adopt guidelines to promote the purchase of environmentally friendly office supplies, such as

- Buy paper, not Styrofoam, drinking cups.
- Use only biodegradable hand soap in school lavatories.
- Insist on recycled paper for school stationery.

It works for Clean Harbors, Inc., in Quincy, Massachusettes.

33. Conduct an autopsy and then hold a moment of silence for any dead ideas you have to bury. It's better than blaming, shaming, and agonizing over mistakes.

34. For every minute late to a meeting, fine the culprit $1 for the "Tardy Kitty." Accumulated proceeds can help finance the next staff party. Credit Linda Miles of Linda Miles and Associates in Virginia Beach, Virginia, for the idea

35. Dare to include your home phone number on communications to parents and the public for use in case of an emergency or dissatisfaction with the responsiveness of other personnel. Surprisingly, you probably won't get many calls; but you will get a lot of credit for credibility and accountability.

36. Hold "Intellectual Food Fights" or "Work-Out" sessions (like a Town Meeting) to work through complex issues. The only rules should be that everyone's ideas count and the only ticket for admission is know-how, not job title. Jack Welch swore by this process when he was in charge of the sprawling General Electric conglomerate.

**CORWIN
PRESS**

The Corwin Press logo—a raven striding across an open book—represents the happy union of courage and learning. We are a professional-level publisher of books and journals for K-12 educators, and we are committed to creating and providing resources that embody these qualities. Corwin's motto is "Success for All Learners."